7

# BRITISH RAILWAYS
## STEAM AND TRACTION IN COLOUR

# Colin Boocock & Brian Morrison

# BRITISH RAILWAYS
## STEAM AND TRACTION IN COLOUR

# BRITISH RAILWAYS IN COLOUR

© Ian Allan Limited 1986

This edition combines two books first
published in 1986 by Ian Allan Limited
under the titles 'B.R. Steam in Colour' (C. Boocock)
and 'B.R. Traction in Colour' (B. Morrison)

ISBN 1 85648 014 3

This edition published 1991 by
The Promotional Reprint Company Limited for
Bookmart Limited (Registered No. 2372865)
Desford Road, Enderby, Leicester, U.K.

Printed in Hong Kong

# CONTENTS

The power of a BR Standard '9F' 2-10-0 is epitomised by this view of No 92058 hammering over Ais Gill with a long southbound freight, one year before the end of steam on BR. *Colour-Rail BRM115*

# THE GLORY OF STEAM 1948-68

It was the sight of a steam locomotive in action that drew so many people into the railway enthusiast community. Lifetimes of devotion to railways resulted from encounters with steam engines; such was the impression of power, of aesthetic form, and of sound engineering. Indeed, surely the steam locomotive represented the ultimate combination in one machine of the art and science of mechanical engineering.

That this was so, is clear because the steam railway engine epitomised the old adage: 'If it looks right, it is right!' History has many instances where the ugly performed less well than the handsome. Compare the performance of the ill-proportioned 'A2' Pacific with the 'A3' or 'A4'; the 'Aberdare' with the '43XX'; the LMS '2P' with a 'T9'; the LNER 'L1' with a BR 2-6-4T. Even so, beauty is in the eye of the beholder, a cliché that was never so true as when applied to steam traction. Controversy rages still over the appearance of Bulleid's 'Q1' 0-6-0, thought by some to be ugly and by others to have a certain plain attractiveness. Many have affection for the simple form of the LNER 'B1' 4-6-0.

How else can one explain the almost universal adoration of all things Great Western? The GW's fleet of engines lacked visual variety and was technically 'safe' rather than up-to-date, but their embellishment with copper and brass decorations set them on pedestals in many men's hearts. Yet the LNER Gresley Pacifics had set new standards in performance as a result of that great engineer's humble acceptance that Chapelon of France could teach a few things, and the LMS pushed ahead with technical developments which extended intervals between repairs and reduced running costs. And even the relatively small Southern Railway had gone further with devices such as steel fireboxes and electric lighting on its technically extraordinary Pacifics.

So steam's glory is expressed in many ways according to one's point of view. It could be the sight of a streamlined 'A4' streaking across the flat Yorkshire plain, or the sound of a 'Duchess' pounding up Camden bank. Maybe the piercing whistle of an LNER 2-6-0 echoing around the mountains near Glenfinnan struck the imagination. Perhaps one was stirred by the steady grind of a 'WD' 2-8-0 hauling stone away from the Derbyshire Peak District, or by the towering billow of steam and smoke that exploded from a Bulleid Pacific as it lost its feet on trying to start its train.

There were, however, those to whom steam engines were less than glorious beasts. Have you ever had to fire a leaky 'H15' 4-6-0 on a heavy Feltham freight in coldest winter? Have your face, eyes, hair, hands, indeed most of you, emerged soot black from a smokebox after cleaning choked boiler fire tubes? Was it your back which ached after lying in a Bulleid 4-6-2's oil bath while you angled yourself to insert the circlips that kept the chain driven valve gear's pins in place? Could you have lived in a house opposite a large engine shed and breathed the smoke-laden atmosphere which blew across from the host of engines being lit up on a Sunday evening ready for next day's services? Or do you, as a passenger, remember that in early British Railways days we did not wear our best clothes when travelling, for fear of getting them marked with the coal dust that penetrated the rolling stock of those years?

Most of us look back in nostalgia, through rose-tinted spectacles, fondly recalling the good moments: the sparkle of Brunswick green paint, the brilliant white steam cloud, the majestic driving wheels, the proud nameplates bearing names of grandeur, the clang of the shovel in the firehole door, the hiss of the steam sanders, the steady acceleration of the deep exhaust beats as the train pulled away. All these are evocative reminders of the giants of steam.

This album is more than a collection of superb pictures journeying into nostalgia. Its chapters trace the path of steam's history during the turbulent first 20 years of the nationalised British Railways. In its pages, discussion ranges over the early decision to build large numbers of new steam locomotives; the success of the standard designs; improvements made to older types. Then the years of change are described, leading to steam's disappearance from the tracks.

If readers can recall their favourite types, remember their happiest journeys, or just wallow in pleasant memories while turning over these pages, this book will have succeeded as a memento of steam's glory.

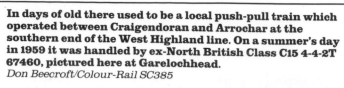

In days of old there used to be a local push-pull train which operated between Craigendoran and Arrochar at the southern end of the West Highland line. On a summer's day in 1959 it was handled by ex-North British Class C15 4-4-2T 67460, pictured here at Garelochhead.
*Don Beecroft/Colour-Rail SC385*

On the St Ives branch line in Cornwall, GW 2-6-2T No 4564 arrives at Carbis Bay towards the end of the 1961 holiday season.   *P. W. Gray/Colour-Rail BRW264*

*Above:*

A happy feature of the last decade of steam on BR was the use in traffic of early locomotives repainted in pre-Grouping (pre-1923) liveries. The restoration was done on the understanding that when the engines were not required for special workings they would be used in normal service. Thus the appearance of 'Jones Goods' 4-6-0 No 103 on a mixed train near Strome Ferry on the Kyle of Lochalsh line was not unusual in 1959! *Derek Cross/Colour-Rail P79*

*Left:*

The most numerous class of steam locomotives in Britain was the ex-GW Class 57XX 0-6-0 pannier tank design, used variously for shunting, freight and local passenger duties. This 1958 view shows No 3600 running round the branch passenger train at Moretonhampstead.
*T. B. Owen/Colour-Rail BRW649*

*Left:*

The rural railway by-way has almost disappeared since this photograph was taken in 1957 of ex-Great Eastern Class D16/3 4-4-0 No 62596 at Gunton with the 9.00am from Gorleston to York. We don't even stack corn like that now!
*E. Alger/Colour-Rail BRE564*

'Rebuilt Scot' No 46108 *Seaforth Highlander* makes a fine picture as it heads an Aberdeen-Manchester train near Howgill. *A. E. R. Cope/Colour-Rail BRM473*

**Ex-works 'Castle' class 4-6-0 No 7022 *Hereford Castle* working the 6.10pm Goodrington-Plymouth meets 2-6-2T No 4561 on a local freight near Aller Junction in July 1960.**
*P. W. Gray/Colour-Rail BRW 189*

*Below:*
**The classic lines of ex-Great Western 'Hall' class 4-6-0
No 4978 *Westwood Hall* glisten in the dark at Newton
Abbot as it pauses while working the 3.30pm parcels train
from Bristol to Plymouth in December 1960.**
*P. W. Gray/Colour-Rail BRW429*

*Bottom:*
**Steam engines displayed unique characteristics at night:
the glare from the open firehole door, swirling steam
reflected in station lights, and sometimes sparks from the
ashpan or chimney. Rebuilt 'Merchant Navy' 4-6-2 No 35026
*Lamport & Holt Line* positively glistens at Southampton
Central as it stands on an up Bournemouth-Waterloo train
in February 1966.** *L. F. Folkard/Colour-Rail BRS232*

# INTRODUCTION
## A Future for Steam?

'Is there a future for steam?' In 1948 it was logical to reach the conclusion that steam traction had a future on British Railways. The argument goes thus.

The four main constituents of BR survived World War 2 with large fleets of steam locomotives totalling over 20,000. While admiring the former independent railways' latest products, young railway engine cleaners also had to attend to locomotives which were as old as were their grandfathers. The newly constituted British Railways could, however, draw on virtually no history of main line diesel traction and had limited diesel railcar experience. Apart from the Southern Region's third rail network, electrification had been limited to some suburban lines in large provincial cities. Money was not in plentiful supply.

With these factors in mind (and with the undoubted advantage of hindsight!) we can envisage a list of options which might have been considered for rejuvenating the locomotive fleet:

Electrify main lines.
Dieselise secondary routes.
Build diesels for shunting.
Design and build new standard steam locomotives.
Adopt as standard the best existing steam types from the 'Big Four' railways.
Continue building Regional types in their current proliferation.

In considering these and other options, the Railway Executive would have recognised that the postwar shortage of capital would preclude widespread electrification at that time. Limited experience of diesel traction in this country would have made general dieselisation a high risk policy. At a time when action was urgent, risks had to be minimised.

So, seen from the situation in which BR found itself in 1948, a decision to continue building steam locomotives would have appeared logical. At the same time, the use of diesels for shunting was already established, and new construction of diesel shunters could be encouraged to the limit of available supply, supplemented by steam types to meet foreseen demands.

What, then, should be the policy for new construction of steam locomotives? Again, circumstances in 1948 should be considered. Each of the Regions had production lines of former designs in full swing at their main workshops. To design and introduce new standard types for BR would take time. It would also take time to test and select standard types from among the former railways' designs. To impose these on other Regions and re-jig their works production to construct and repair unfamiliar types could have been counter-productive.

So logic indicated that BR should, in the short term, go on building existing types in the Regions' workshops and at contractors, at least until a longer-term policy could be established. In fact, an early decision was taken to design and introduce as soon as possible a range of new standard steam locomotives of low-risk, simple designs that would meet all Regions' future motive power requirements. These standard steam types would have lower maintenance costs, would in time displace the Regional designs, and would in their turn eventually be displaced by hoped-for future electrification of main lines supported by selective dieselisation of other routes when enough experience had been gained of the new types of traction.

Meanwhile, the LNER and Southern Railway in particular had bequeathed BR such an array of old fashioned, outdated engines on branch line, shunting and light mixed traffic duties that an interim policy was adopted in these cases. Modern, LMS-designed locomotives were delivered in some numbers to these areas until equivalent BR standard designs were available. In particular one recalls the Southern Region's use of Fairburn 2-6-4Ts, built at Brighton works to replace pre-Grouping (1923) designs, and the spread of Ivatt 2-6-0s into the North Eastern Region and on to the Midland & Great Northern section of the Eastern.

From 1951, in a remarkably short timescale, appeared the new BR Standard types. They met their principal objectives well, and some were indeed brilliant performers. Others needed improvements which are documented later in this book.

By the early 1950s, motive power policy was beginning to evolve towards fundamental change. Firstly, the advantages of diesel railcars had been grasped, and from 1953 these appeared in large numbers, putting into question the futures of some of the recently built branch line steam classes. When the 1955 Modernisation Plan was announced by the Conservative government of the day, the *Sunday Express* ran the banner headline: 'The End of the Steam Train!' In 1957 came the pilot main line diesels, followed, more quickly than had been planned, by large builds of new diesel locomotives for general main line mixed traffic use.

These new orders for diesels sounded the death knell for new steam locomotive construction, though it took a couple of years to stop building steam for good. Certainly, the Modernisation Plan did not herald the immediate cessation of construction of steam locomotives. Indeed some works, such as Swindon, produced new steam and diesel locomotives alongside one another for some years. History records that No 92220 *Evening Star* left Swindon Works in 1960, to bring new steam construction for British Railways to its end.

Technically, BR steam locomotive development had not stood still during these years. Improvements had been made to several types, including favourites like the 'Castles' and 'A3s', and major projects such as the rebuilding of the Bulleid Pacifics had been undertaken.

However, a major event, foreshadowed by another newspaper's headline, 'Dr Beeching's Pill', was to change the life-span of the entire steam fleet, and was even to change the prospects of some of the diesels as well. BR's chairman, Dr Richard Beeching (later Lord Beeching) began asking questions about the economic size of the railway system, and got some controversial answers. In the years following 1962, many miles of under-utilised railway, duplicate routes and lightly used stations and goods yards were closed. The demand for locomotives was suddenly cut back, and the wholesale scrapping of steam traction which followed has no comparison in British railway history, not even with the Great Western's withdrawal of its broad gauge engines, itself also a late reaction to inevitable market forces. Thus, the latest '9Fs' which were new in 1960 had all gone by 1968. Bulleid Pacifics, on which considerable sums had been spent in rebuilding, had no more than 10, and sometimes as little as four years to recover these costs by savings in maintenance and fuel consumption. And even some diesels which were new in the late 1950s had found their way to scrapyards by the late 1960s.

In 1967, British Rail had only one main line still using steam to haul express passenger trains. The Southern had planned its Bournemouth electrification to be completed in 1967, and on 9 July that year the last express steam train, hauled by a Bulleid Pacific, reached its Waterloo. The next year, railway enthusiasts went on pilgrimages to places such as Carnforth and Lostock Hall to witness the last months of steam haulage of freight and local passenger services on the London Midland Region, and on BR. Familiar 'Black 5s', '8Fs', and BR 4-6-0s clanked across the hills with their loads.

Then suddenly it was all over.

**One of the last 'Jubilees' in service, No 45562 *Alberta* makes a fine sight passing Grayrigg with the 'Border Countryman' special in February 1967.** *A. E. R. Cope/Colour-Rail BRM478*

Stanier 'Black 5' No 45130 stands at Bangor, North Wales, in 1956 with a down express.  *J. H. Moss/Colour-Rail BRM816*

*Right:*
**This picture of Gresley Class A3 Pacific No 60111 *Enterprise* drifting light through Grantham in summer 1962 illustrates the beautifully balanced lines of this class. No 60111 had been fitted with new cylinders and a double exhaust.**
*Colin Boocock*

*Above:*
**The tranquility of the rural railway is portrayed by Class 14XX 0-4-2T No 1450 propelling a single auto-coach from Bampton to Exeter, as recently as 1963.**
*T. B. Owen/Colour-Rail BRW456*

*Left:*
**The grace of steam is illustrated by this 1959 view of spotless Great Western 4-6-0 No 7811 *Dunley Manor* near Bow Street on the up 'Cambrian Coast Express'.**
*T. B. Owen/Colour-Rail BRW552*

*Above:*

The massive variety of pre-Grouping locomotives ensured that many were confined to their home localities. At Craigellachie No 62262, a 4-4-0 of the former Great North of Scotland Railway, is in charge of a freight for Aviemore in **August 1954.** *E. S. Russell/Colour-Rail SC165*

*Below:*

The Great Western 'Kings' did excellent work on the Birmingham line. 4-6-0 No 6012 *King Edward VI* was photographed near Beaconsfield in April 1962 heading the 11.00am Birmingham Snow Hill-Paddington.
*P. Mullett/Colour-Rail BRW330*

*Top:*
**Rebuilt 'Royal Scot' 4-6-0 No 46142 *The York & Lancaster Regiment* scuttles through the Lune gorge on the West Coast main line in June 1963.**
*M. Chapman/Colour-Rail BRM567*

*Above:*
**The hobby of train spotting reached its zenith in the 1960s; it dropped significantly after the end of steam in 1968. A new generation of modern traction enthusiasts has lately revived the hobby, and has resumed the practice of gathering at the lineside to watch their favourites, such as these spotters were doing back in 1960 as Stanier 'Princess Royal' 4-6-2 No 46207 *Princess Arthur of Connaught* passed Bushey with the up 'Ulster Express'.**
*T. B. Owen/Colour-Rail BRM666*

*Above:*
**In east Lancashire, Stanier LMS 2-6-4T No 42460 enters Colne with a stopping train from Blackburn.**
*G. Warnes/Colour-Rail BRM583*

*Below:*
**Heavy summer holiday trains in the West Country needed two engines to be able to surmount the banks. Ex-GW 4-6-0s Nos 7813 *Freshford Manor* and 6832 *Brockton Grange* head 16 coaches from Newquay across the lattice viaduct at Largin in September 1958.**
*T. B. Owen/Colour-Rail BRW445*

*Top:*
**The Southern's 'Lord Nelson' 4-6-0s performed competently if not outstandingly on the Bournemouth expresses and Southampton boat trains. One of these popular machines brings a Bournemouth-Waterloo train into Winchester.**
*Colin Boocock*

*Above:*
**In this busy evening scene at Perth, 'Rebuilt Scot' No 46166 *London Rifle Brigade* has arrived with a down express and Class 5 No 44997 waits to take over for the assault of the Highland main line towards Inverness. A former Caledonian tank simmers by the side of the station.**
*W. J. V. Anderson/Colour-Rail SC123*

# ONE

# EXPRESS INHERITANCE

It is a brave man who can stand up amid a railway gathering and pronounce definitively which class of top express locomotive was the best inherited by British Railways in 1948. The 'A4s', 'Duchesses'. 'Merchant Navies' and 'Kings' all had their individual best features.

Foremost in terms of maximum speed were the LNER 'A4s', with *Mallard* holding the world speed record of 126mph. Sir Nigel Gresley had gifted his streamlined 4-6-2s with scientifically profiled aerofoil curves to reduce air resistance at high speed, a powerful, free-steaming boiler for sustained high output, and large cross-section steam and exhaust passages to ensure efficient steam distribution and exhaust release. His conjugated inside valve gear, subject to overrun when worn, and the propensity for the inside big end to overheat were the only significant faults of an intelligently evolved design.

The LMS matched the 'A4' with a slightly bigger brute with four cylinders which produced a theoretically greater tractive effort. The 'Duchesses' were at least as well suited to hard slog as they were to high speed, but nonetheless one of the streamlined version was once pushed to 114mph near Crewe. In the 1948 locomotive exchanges, when the best engines of each of the former railways were tested on each others' routes, the LMS '8P' Pacifics recorded the most economical performances, though not the most startling running. The 'Duchesses' and their sister 'Cities' performed reliably, hauling enormous length trains on the West Coast main line to Glasgow over Shap and Beattock summits, sometimes reaching as far north as Perth. They were Britain's biggest Pacifics.

The Southern Railway also had heavy loads to pull over very difficult, hilly roads such as those from London to Dover and to Exeter via Salisbury. Bulleid's provision for the SR of the 'Merchant Navy' class 4-6-2s presented that railway with a class of very high performers, capable of exceptionally high boiler outputs, speeds of over 100mph (with 6ft 2in wheels!) and many modern features. His steel fireboxes proved to be a highly successful feature. With controlled water treatment they were very easy on firebox maintenance. Drivers liked the enclosed cabs and electric lighting and the thoughtful placing of the controls within easy reach of the driving position. The locomotives'

countless mechanical innovations, such as chain-driven valve gear in an oil bath, flat plate smokebox and fabricated chimney, steam reverse and steam-powered firehole door, seriously reduced the reliability of these handsome machines. The valve gear in particular used to overrun and cut-off late at high speeds, a major cause of heavy fuel and water consumption (and the cause of the myth that they were very free running at high speed!). Nonetheless their running was frequently brilliant, and particularly so in the 1948 exchanges where economy was sacrificed against high power outputs.

The Great Western had relied on its 'King' class 4-6-0s since 1927. Very handsome indeed, and extremely powerful for a 4-6-0 design, with normal loads they edged into the performance league represented by the other railways' largest Pacific types. The 'Kings' were, after all, the oldest '8P' locomotives and their narrow fireboxes must have been a limitation to absolute maximum power. Their greater width across the cylinders prevented their trial over more than the GW and LNER main lines in 1948, and the Pacifics really held the limelight at that time.

When British Railways had decided on standard colours to paint their stock, all these magnificent, inherited, top-link machines from the 'Big Four' railways received a strong blue livery with black and white lining-out, overlaid on the tenders with the smart new lion-over-wheel emblem of BR. Coupled to red and cream coaches, these engines all looked superb, and attracted a great deal of admiration. Blue was a natural colour anyway for an 'A4'. It equally suited the air-smoothed 'Merchant Navy' and the bulk of a Stanier 'Duchess'. A blue 'King' was a novelty, certainly, in many opinions a handsome one, but diehard opinion preferred GWR Brunswick green!

Later, British Railways decided that the blue did not wear well (the author has no recollection of this actually being the case) and the locomotives were subsequently repainted in BR Brunswick green at their next overhaul. While the 'Kings' and 'Merchant Navies' still looked fine in green, the 'Duchesses' looked less strong and the 'A4s' partially lost their appeal.

Brunswick green had already been applied to the railways' other express engines, too, down through the lesser 4-6-2s ('A3s', 'A2s', 'West Countries') and the 4-6-0s as low as power class 5P. Thus the Southern's splendid 'King Arthurs' were green, and so were the 'B17s', 'Jubilees', rebuilt 'Royal Scots', 'Lord Nelsons' and 'Castles'.

The '7P' range was a mixed bunch of types, typified by the 'Castles', 'Lord Nelsons' and 'Royal Scots'. The 1948 exchanges pitted 'West Country' Pacifics as the Southern's entries in the mixed traffic range, but the smaller LMS 'Royal Scots' had to perform against the '8P' giants. In Scotland the SR's light Pacific amazed the locals with its haulage exploits over the Highland main line. On the SR these engines often deputised competently for their bigger 'Merchant Navy' sisters, though they suffered from most of the bigger engines' design difficulties.

The 'Castles' were the mainstay of Western Region main line services and performed with economy and distinction even when driven quite hard. They were more of a racehorse breed than a heavy haulage machine, and double-heading was very common on the steeper banks in the West.

The similarity in size between a 'Castle' and a 'Lord Nelson' is clearly evident. The 'Nelsons' were in many ways of sewing machine quality mechanically, and were extremely reliable. However, their very long fireboxes were difficult to fire successfully. Eastleigh depot men made well with them on Southampton boat trains as they were well suited to that depot's light-handed handling of its steeds. Demonstration of the heavy haulage ability of a 'Lord Nelson' however has had to wait until the 1980s and the preservation era! That is another story.

The LMS bequeathed to BR its large fleet of 'Royal Scots', still being rebuilt with taper boilers, a programme which BR went on to complete. The 'Royal Scots' had originally been built with an eye on the 'Lord Nelson' design for guidance. Why the 'Scots' needed rebuilding and the 'LNs' did not is a question few Derby men would answer, one fears! That is a particularly poignant point because the smaller 'Patriots' apparently performed satisfactorily (even though BR initially painted them black), and indeed the later 'Jubilee' 4-6-0s were barely distinguishable in the consistency of their performance. In good hands the 'Jubilees' put up some sparkling performances, particularly on the main line out of St Pancras. Heavy loads on that route demanded double heading however; the London Midland Region sorely needed bigger engines.

A big engine policy had already provided the LNER with a large fleet of Pacifics of 'A2', A3' and 'A4' types, and the 'A1' design appeared on the scene just after Nationalisation. (Indeed one newspaper was seen to comment that the first BR Standard engine had appeared!) Mr Peppercorn's three-cylinder simple Pacific was a splendid, basic machine, stronger than an 'A4' and without its mechanical weaknesses. The 'A1s' were indeed handsome and worked heavy trains from King's Cross to Leeds, York and Newcastle with ease. The problems with the 'A2' 4-6-2s have been well documented elsewhere, but in reality their running could often match their larger-wheeled Peppercorn sisters. They found very useful employment particularly over Scotland's hilly main lines. The Gresley 'A3s' likewise put up fine performances, often only slightly inferior to the bigger machines.

However, the LNER had left a considerable tract of its territory with its express trains underpowered. The Great Eastern lines to Norwich and Cambridge had nothing bigger than the Gresley three-cylinder 'B17' 4-6-0s or their Thompson two-cylinder 'B2' equivalents to haul the express trains, which meant that speeds were not high, particularly on the difficult Norwich route. Equally, the Southern did not have enough Pacifics to cover all heavy trains, and many passengers to Ramsgate and Dover found their 12-coach trains headed by nothing bigger than a 'Schools' class 4-4-0. Even though these engines were the biggest 4-4-0s in Europe, and also were technically excellent and efficient engines, they were not big enough for much that they had to do, and timings on the Kent lines were slow in consequence. BR at first did not even think of them as being worthy of green livery. They were painted black, with LNW-style red, cream and grey lining, and when clean they looked very smart indeed; not an express livery though!

So British Railways' express inheritance was a group of highly competent top-link classes between which any logical choice was difficult, and a wide mixture of second and third range types (7P, 6P and 5P power classes), only a few of which were really modern and most of which had characteristics unsuitable for adoption as the basis for standard BR designs.

For example, neither the 'Castles' nor the 'Lord Nelsons' were modern designs. The 'Royal Scots' were no real match for the '7P' 4-6-2s which the Southern and LNER possessed. Yet the 'West Country' and 'Battle of Britain' class possessed Bulleid's engineering features, the 'A2s' sometimes rode indifferently and were strictly of main line route availability, and the 'A3' lineage dated from the Great Northern Railway's 'A1' class of 1922. Also, the 'King Arthur' and 'B17'/'B2' classes were completely outclassed by more modern mixed traffic types.

BR's perceived need therefore was for higher powered locomotives on the secondary main lines of Britain. How this need was eventually met emerges in later chapters.

Incidentally, the London Midland Region did solve the problem of the unsatisfactory appearance of 'Duchesses' in green. By adopting a maroon colour, reminiscent of the former LMS red, the looks of these great engines were transformed, as illustrations in this book testify.

The fastest steam locomotives to be inherited by British Railways were without doubt the Gresley 'A4' Pacifics. No 60008 *Dwight D. Eisenhower* shows off its curves while standing near the coaling plant at King's Cross depot.
*P. Mullett/Colour-Rail BRE270*

*Above:*
Gresley's 'A3' class were fine looking locomotives. No 60093 *Coronach* is seen in original form at Edinburgh at the head of a Waverley route express to Carlisle.
*J. G. Wallace/Colour-Rail SC427*

*Left:*
The Southern bequeathed the solid and reliable 'King Arthur' class 4-6-0s to British Railways, exemplified by No 30794 *Sir Ector de Maris*, photographed in January 1959 passing Pirbright Junction with a down Southampton Docks boat train.   *T. B. Owen/Colour-Rail BRS397*

*Left:*
The Southern 'Schools' were the largest 4-4-0s in Europe. No 30927 *Clifton* leaves Dover under the white cliffs near Shakespeare tunnel with an up express in 1958. Electrification displaced these fine engines four years later.   *T. B. Owen/Colour-Rail BRS452*

*Top:*
**The fine appearance of Maunsell's four-cylinder 'Lord Nelson' class 4-6-0s is displayed by this view at Eastleigh depot of No 30863 *Lord Rodney*.** *Colin Boocock*

*Above:*
**The handsome lines of ex-Great Western 'King' 4-6-0 No 6011 *King James I* (at Bath Spa in 1950) are emphasised by BR's early blue livery, illustrated in this rare colour slide. Most people preferred the former Brunswick green, to which BR reverted around 1950.**
*Kenneth Leech/Colour-Rail BRW329*

*Left:*

**The Thompson rebuilds of Gresley's 'P2' 2-8-2s into 'A2/2' class 4-6-2s were not entirely successful, and the locomotives were withdrawn from service early. Near the end of its life, No 60506 *Wolf of Badenoch* was photographed in August 1959 on an up express near Eaton Wood.** *P. J. Hughes/Colour-Rail BRE256*

*Left:*

**Crossing the river Clyde at Crawford in September 1964 is 'Rebuilt Scot' 4-6-0 No 46140 *The King's Royal Rifle Corps* at the head of a down express.**
*A. E. R. Cope/Colour-Rail SC220*

*Below:*

**The massive bulk of 'Princess Royal' 4-6-2 No 46208 *Princess Helena Victoria* is dressed overall in experimental red livery at Camden depot in February 1959.**
*T. B. Owen/Colour-Rail BRM469*

*Above:*
**Rebuilt 'Patriot' 4-6-0 No 45532 *Illustrious* heads a down express near Lancaster in 1962.**
*A. E. R. Cope/Colour-Rail BRM171*

*Below:*
**Thankfully, black exhausts such as is emitting here from 'Patriot' 4-6-0 No 45519 *Lady Godiva* were rare. The engine is rounding the curve at Dore & Totley in June 1960.**
*P. J. Hughes/Colour-Rail BRM496*

*Above:*
**Gresley three-cylinder 4-6-0 No 61620 *Clumber* of Class B17/6 passes Chaloners Whin with a York-Hull train in May 1957.** *W. Oliver/Colour-Rail BRE204*

*Below:*
**The LMS 'Jubilee' 4-6-0s were handsome beasts even when paired with the early, narrow Fowler tenders! Birmingham New Street is host to No 45740 *Munster* preparing to leave with an express for Euston in September 1956.** *T. J. Edgington/Colour-Rail BRM294*

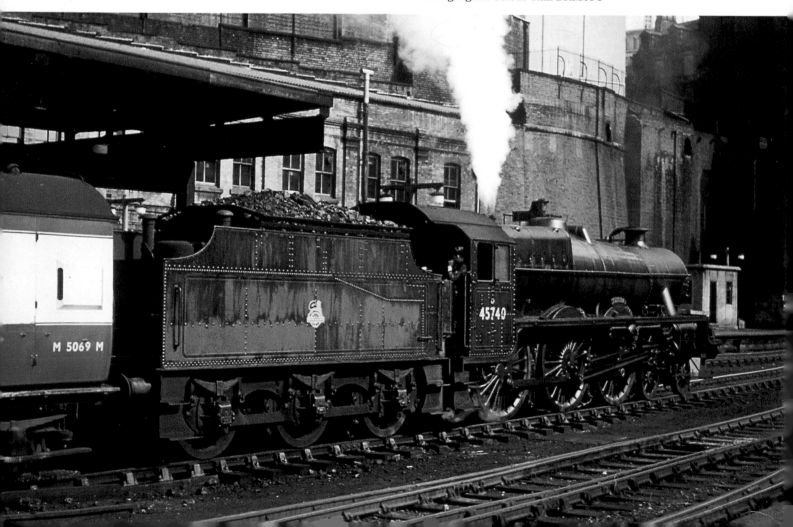

# TWO

# MIXED TRAFFIC MEDLEY

More LMS Class 5 4-6-0s were built than any other tender locomotive class in Britain. A simple, basic, medium sized engine with Swindonian boiler proportions and a good steam distribution and exhaust arrangement, the 'Black 5' was used on any and every type of traffic. They worked express passenger trains to Blackpool, heavy freight over Shap, local stopping trains to Bournemouth and Wick, tourist trains to Kyle of Lochalsh and boat trains to Holyhead.

It is not surprising therefore that such a useful general-purpose loocomotive type had, in general layout, been arrived at by the other companies also. The Great Western 'Hall' class and the 'Modified Hall' derivative performed the same range of tasks within the Western Region. The LNER 'B1' was another similarly laid-out design which met the same need in the east of the country, similar in size to the earlier North Eastern Railway 'B16' 4-6-0s. The Southern had its Maunsell 'H15' 4-6-0s as well, though being derived from a much older design they were not in the same class as the other railways' designs as regards performance.

Above the Class 5 power range, the former railways had gone in differing directions in the mixed traffic field. The LNER had its 'V2' 2-6-2s, a large class of big Gresley machines whose performance often approached that expected of his Pacific locomotives. Indeed the 'V2' design formed the basis of some of the 'A2' class, which was ostensibly a mixed traffic type but which mostly kept to passenger trains.

The LMS had no mixed traffic engine bigger than a Class 5, but the Great Western did produce one larger 4-6-0 type, the 'County' class with 6ft 3in wheels, which again spent most of its life in passenger workings. On the other hand, the '47XX' 2-8-0 engines were basically freight machines which performed as required on passenger extras at summer weekends, as did the SR's 'S15' class 4-6-0s. That the Bulleid light Pacifics were officially mixed traffic was not often taken up in real life.

Every railway had 2-6-0s of a 'go anwhere' specification. Indeed the LMS 'Crabs' and the Stanier equivalents were power class 5, and the LNER 'K3' (Gresley) and 'K1' (Thompson) were strong, rugged beasts as well. The Great Western and the Southern had Moguls of a similar size but different in layout: the '43XX' was a small but strong performer, with inside valve gear; the SR

used their outside valve geared 'N' and 'U', and the three-cylinder 'N1' and 'U1' 2-6-0s universally around the Region on all types of traffic up to but not including express trains (if one excludes the Lymington boat trains from that description!). A near match for the '43XX' was the GW 'Manor' class 4-6-0, and slightly larger was the 'Grange' design. With these three types and the 'Hall' 4-6-0, the GW had a strangely close-stepped range of engines, a closeness followed later, surprisingly, among BR's Standard designs. The LNER 'K2' and 'K4' 2-6-0s were ubiquitous in the west of Scotland, the LMS had its modern Ivatt Class 4 2-6-0s and the Southern retained the small class of LB&SCR 'K' 2-6-0s.

When one comes to survey mixed traffic designs of power classes 3 and 2, one finds a virtual dearth of small tender engines specially built for mixed traffic duties. True enough, older freight and passenger locomotives, particularly pre-Grouping ones, often performed mixed traffic turns on branch lines, but to the author's recall only the LMS actually built a new design of small mixed traffic tender locomotive, the Ivatt Class 2 2-6-0. This was intended to enable old branch line engines such as Kirtley 2-4-0s and LNW 'Cauliflowers' to be replaced; which was a laudable objective. Whether it was economic to sink scarce capital into engines destined to work low-traffic and thus by inference uneconomic routes, can be questioned with hindsight. One can assume that the state of the oldest engines at that time rendered such a course inevitable, there being no dieselisation policy north of the GWR.

Which was the most successful mixed traffic class of engine inherited by BR? This is an exceptionally difficult question to answer. In terms of performance, the 'V2' was in a class of its own. However, to compare a 'Black 5' with a 'B1' and a 'Hall' is to talk in shades of grey. No doubt the running of the 'Halls' and Class 5s on the Chester-Birkenhead joint line gave rise to comparisons. Any differences were more likely to be due to the Stephenson and Walschaerts valve gear characteristics than to overall engine and boiler dimensions. Enginemen in Scotland who drove both Class 5s and 'B1s' often said they liked the liveliness of the 'B1s' acceleration on passenger trains, but preferred the 'Black 5s' for hard slogging. The closeness of the merits of these 4-6-0s appears to have led to an interesting compromise in the design of the BR Standard 4-6-0s, which is developed in the appropriate chapter.

Comparison of 2-6-0s in the power class 4 range having a wide field of operation leads us to look at the GWR '43XX', the LMS Ivatt Class 4 2-6-0, the Southern 'N' and 'U' family, and the LNER 'K2' and 'K4' types. All these, other than the Ivatt engines, were based on pre-1923 designs. The 'N' and 'U' were possibly the most modern in concept of these older designs. Construction of an additional number of 'N' class 2-6-0s had been chosen as a post-World War 1 national project at Woolwich Arsenal to relieve unemployment. They were two-cylinder simples with large piston valves and Swindon-style taper boilers. Very strong for their size in terms of their ability to move quite heavy loads briskly, they were slightly under-boilered as a compromise to achieve wider route availability. Examples from the Woolwich build had found their

way to Ireland and Egypt and to the Metropolitan Railway (as 2-6-4Ts), as well as to augment the Southern Railway's own fleet.

However, it was natural that the LMS Ivatt design, being a very free steaming, reliable, lively performer with expectation of long intervals between maintenance and shopping, was regarded by many as the star type in this power range. Some did suggest that its 5ft 3in wheels tended to cause it to become mechanically worn prematurely. Many would thus have liked to have seen a 5ft 8in tender version of the successful Stanier and Fairburn 2-6-4T instead, but this opportunity was not taken up.

The smaller engines were not subjected to the moderate rigours of the 1948 locomotive exchanges programme. In the light of the foregoing discussion, however, BR's choice for future construction proved to be predictable.

Mixed traffic engines were ideal for secondary routes such as in the Scottish highlands. LNER Class K1/1 2-6-0 No 61997 *MacCailin Mor* brings a down freight train along the West Highland line near Glenfinnan.
*D. M. C. Hepburne-Scott/Colour-Rail SC401*

The early 'B1's were named, mainly after breeds of deer, hence the class's nickname 'Bongos'! No 61018 *Gnu* pauses at Sleights in May 1964 with a pick-up freight for Whitby. *J. M. Boyes/Colour-Rail BRE199*

The most useful mixed traffic locomotives on the Southern Region were Maunsell's series of numerous 2-6-0s. One of the rarer three-cylinder varieties, Class U1 No 31898, leaves Southampton Central station with the daily through train from Brighton to Plymouth in September 1957.

B. J. Swain/Colour-Rail BRS414

*Below:*

**The Somerset & Dorset climbed the Mendips in both
directions, often necessitating double-heading of the
heaviest trains. Two former S&D locomotives, '4F' No 44560
and '7F' No 53806 head the empty stock of a pigeon special,
including stock of LMS and GWR origins, at Evercreech
New in August 1962.**   *P. Mullett/Colour-Rail SD77*

*Bottom:*

**In this period scene (August 1959) Class K2/2 2-6-0 No 61787
*Loch Quoich* poses at the old Fort William station. 'K2s' and
'K4s' were the mainstay of the West Highland line
passenger and freight services for many years.**
*R. E. Toop/Colour-Rail SC326*

*Above:*
**4-6-0 No 6879 *Overton Grange* is seen at the head of a down freight near Widney Manor in June 1963.**
*M. Mensing/Colour-Rail BRW441*

*Left:*
**The Great Western introduced the 'County' class 4-6-0s after World War 2. No 1010 *County of Caernarvon* is near Harbury with a down express to Birmingham in July 1963.**
*A. E. R. Cope/Colour-Rail BRW131*

*Left:*
**GW 4-6-0 No 5940 *Whitbourne Hall* faces Plymouth as it awaits departure from Newton Abbot.**
*P. W. Gray/Colour-Rail BRW203*

35

Stanier Class 5 4-6-0 No 45308 was photographed at Manchester Victoria one December evening in 1961.

*N. Harrop/Colour-Rail BRM339*

# THREE

# 'BIG FOUR' FREIGHT

In the early days of British Railways, freight trains were typically quite heavy but ran at slow speeds. Usually wagons were small and numerous, and most were not fitted with continuous brakes. This necessitated a brake van at the rear of each train so that the guard could apply the handbrake on his van whenever it was necessary to slow down or to control the train on down-grades. This meant that, on the part of the engine driver, handling of goods trains required gentle acceleration and deceleration, with careful application and release of brakes, in order to avoid snatching of couplings and the possibility of buffer locking or even derailment.

Steam locomotives designed specifically for this type of work characteristically had small coupled wheels for high tractive effort and low speed; more wheels for better adhesion and braking; and relatively moderate boiler power because gentle acceleration did not demand great power outputs.

As a result, the biggest 2-8-0 freight locomotives on the three former railways which dealt with heavy freight (GW, LMS and LNE), although classified '8F' and of high tractive effort, carried boilers little bigger than did other engines of power class 5P or 5MT.

In the 1948 exchanges the LMS '8F' was pitted against the LNER 'O1' 2-8-0, the WD 2-8-0 and 2-10-0 designs and the '28XX' from the Western. The latter proved particularly successful, all the more so bearing in mind its 1903 Churchward origins. The purpose of setting up this group of trials was less clear, because the 2-8-0 type was already available in large numbers. The acquisition of over 700 War Department 2-8-0s after World War 2 virtually eliminated the need for any new construction of heavy, slow-speed freight engines.

Another feature of lower speed operation was its relative kindness to mechanical parts. Freight engines accumulated mileage over a much longer time than did passenger or mixed traffic types. Longevity was not therefore unusual. This was demonstrated notably on the North Eastern Region where the pre-Grouping NER 0-8-0s of Classes Q6 and Q7 survived on coal traffic right through to dieselisation without being replaced by more modern types of steam traction. Similarly the former Great Central 2-8-0s (and their LNER successors) on the Eastern Region were to survive into the 1960s hauling the products of the Yorkshire coalfield. The North Eastern 'J27' 0-6-0s,

heavy engines for that wheel arrangement, also lasted through to dieselisation.

The Southern Railway had three main groups of heavy freight traffic. Cross-London transfer freight was largely in the hands of big tank engines, the ex-LSW 4-8-0T and 4-6-2T engines of massive Urie dimensions, supplemented by Maunsell Class W 2-6-4Ts that were to all intents and purposes tank versions of the 'N1' class. Another group covered the trunk haulage of goods to and from the great docks of Southampton and the other south coast ports. There was also coal traffic from the Kent coalfield, and the usual general distribution of goods and fuel around the Region's territory.

The Southampton Docks freights were exclusively in the capable hands of Maunsell 'S15' 4-6-0s, a design which any other Region would have classified as mixed traffic. Many of these freights were fully vacuum braked, and the 5ft 6in wheels of these hard slogging engines suited their purpose well.

For general freight, O. V. S. Bulleid had supplied the SR with his 40 'Q1' class 0-6-0s. These, and the 20 earlier Maunsell 'Qs', were good, reliable machines.

At the top end of the power spectrum were the LMS Beyer-Garratt 2-6-0+0-6-2Ts. These had been built to eliminate double heading of heavy coal trains such as those which ran from Toton in Nottinghamshire to Brent in north London. The Garratts looked enormous to British eyes, and their qualities have recently been well documented. Suffice it to summarise here, that if their makers' recommendations on steam and exhaust distribution arrangements had been adhered to, they might well have been highly successful performers.

Enormity also appeared in the LNER's Garratt, the 2-8-0+0-8-2T which banked coal trains and heavy freight on the Worsborough incline near Mexborough, before the route was electrified as part of the Manchester-Sheffield-Wath scheme. This locomotive was in effect two Gresley 'O2' 2-8-0s fed by one enormous boiler. One regrets that Britain's liking for slow speeds and loose coupled trains had not encouraged development of a fleet of these. The other giant banker of note, of course, was the Midland's 0-10-0 which assisted trains up the 1 in 37 of the Lickey incline.

At the lower end of the scale, all railways had a host of 0-6-0s of various sizes, the typical British local goods engine in fact. Probably there was not a great deal to choose between most of them, but it is sensible to pick out the GWR's Collett '2251' class for special mention. This type was ostensibly the only 'modern' 0-6-0 outside the Southern Region, and was a particularly good design. It was certainly capable of normal goods work, but it also had a surprising turn of speed, aided by unusually excellent riding qualities for an engine of that arrangement. Thus it found itself quite at home on local passenger duties, more so than many other 0-6-0s which were often pressed into passenger service. For example, one recalls the '4Fs' being driven over the Mendip hills on the Somerset & Dorset line local trains neither running very well nor always steaming all that freely — and producing some extremely metallic noises from their mechanisms!

Other freight engine types which were drafted on to passenger trains were relatively rare, other than on lightly laid branches. The S&DJR '7F' 2-8-0s were excellent machines for taking up to 10 coaches unaided over the Mendips during summer Saturdays, but other 2-8-0s such as 'WDs' and '8Fs', 'O4s' and '28XXs' did not normally deviate from hauling freight traffic. Another exception was the Western's '47XX' 2-8-0 which appeared on holiday extras in the summer months.

Interestingly, BR saw fit not to design any new pure freight engines at all, other than to fill the yawning gap at the top end of the power range. Fast fitted freights up to the year 1950 or so required either mixed traffic engines such as LMS Class 5s, or even bigger machines like the LNER Pacifics and 'V2s'. Six-coupled engines were a serious limitation to the loads which could be started. BR's answer to this need was to be one of the most successful types ever designed for a British railway.

**The 'WD' 2-8-0s were the most numerous freight engines on British Railways. No 90243 heads a train of limestone hoppers near Dent in June 1966.**
*A. E. R. Cope/Colour-Rail BRM548*

The Great Central Railway's Robinson 2-8-0 freight design was selected to be a war engine for overseas service in World War 1. A number subsequently survived on the Great Western as Class ROD. The majority, nearly four hundred, lived their lives on their home territory in Yorkshire, Lincolnshire and Nottinghamshire. Class O4/3 No 63782 plugs steadily along the up loop line at Eaton Wood in June 1959. *P. J. Hughes/Colour-Rail BRE308*

*Left:*
The Midland Railway's unique four-cylinder 0-10-0 'Big Bertha' had a long and noisy life shoving trains up the 1 in 37 Lickey incline. As BR No 58100 it is seen banking a freight near the summit at Blackwell in 1954.
*C. Banks collection/Colour-Rail BRM821*

*Left:*
The North-east coalfield freights were ably handled by ex-North Eastern Railway motive power right through to dieselisation. Class Q7 0-8-0 No 63471 is seen in September 1960 heading a freight away from Tyne Dock.
*T. B. Owen/Colour-Rail BRE438*

Not only were the 'WD' 2-10-0s Riddles' most successful overseas war locomotive design, their arrangement of coupled axle side play was adopted for BR's '9F' 2-10-0 to guarantee its route availability. Twenty five 'WD' 2-10-0s were put to work in Scotland after the war, of which No 90773 was pictured at Grangemouth shed in June 1962.

*P. Mullett/Colour-Rail SC420*

'Grange' 4-6-0 No 6861 *Crynant Grange* enters Birmingham
Snow Hill station with an up freight.
*T. J. Edgington/Colour-Rail BRW212*

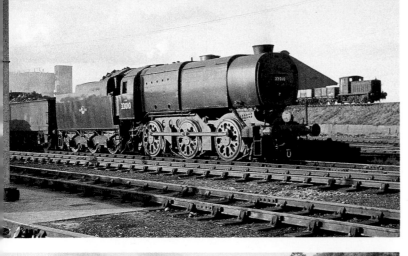

*Left:*

**The starkly simple lines of Bulleid's 'Q1' class 0-6-0s are well illustrated by this view of No 33010 at Hither Green shed in 1963. Their design was aimed at reducing to a minimum the amount of metal and effort required in their construction.** *Colin Boocock*

*Left:*

**The Midland Railway's small engine policy bequeathed to the LMS nothing larger than the '4F' 0-6-0 for freight, although the LMS went on to build many more of them! No 43935 approaches Miller's Dale station with a stopping train from Derby to Manchester Central in 1963.** *Colin Boocock*

*Below:*

**A pair of ex-Caledonian 0-6-0s pulls away from Annbank in the Ayrshire coalfield. These engines were typical examples of the most common type of goods locomotive in Britain. Virtually all pre-Grouping railways possessed medium weight 0-6-0s such as these.** *Derek Cross/Colour-Rail SC58*

*Above:*
**So useful were the ex-LNWR Class G1 0-8-0s that rebuilding of them to Class G2a with higher boiler pressure continued well into the BR period. No 49350 is pictured on Western Region territory at Oxford shed.**
*Don Beecroft/Colour-Rail BRW724*

*Below:*
**There were over 600 of Stanier's highly successful '8F' class 2-8-0 design. Two, Nos 48352 and 48471, double-head a civil engineers' train at Low Gill.**
*J. Davenport/Colour-Rail BRM829*

# FOUR

# SMALLER FRY

One of the results of continuous steam locomotive development over 140 years was the production of bigger and bigger engines, culminating in the express passenger machines described in an earlier chapter. As each new top link design appeared, so were earlier express passenger engines relegated to lower links. The express locomotives of the 1920s were by 1948 handling secondary main line work, and the survivors of those built between 1890 and 1920 were distinctly non-express in their daily employment!

The Great Eastern '1500s' (Class B12), Highland 'Castles', GN and LB&SC Atlantics, LSW 'Paddleboxes', LNW 'Prince of Wales' and 'Claughtons' were typically on stopping train duties. Midland 'Compounds', Drummond 'T9s', GE 'Claud Hamiltons', indeed the whole group of middle sized 4-4-0s, found themselves on lighter, local or cross-country line services. The LMS '2Ps' provided power to assist 'Jubilees' on St Pancras-Manchester expresses; so propelled, they reached 90mph on occasions, but their other duties were far more menial.

Since virtually every pre-1923 railway had taken part in this development of express power, there had emerged a plethora of different, if conceptually similar, designs based on the 4-4-0 layout. The norm was two inside cylinders, inside valve gear, and driving wheels of 6ft 6in to 7ft 0in diameter. Early engines were saturated, later ones had superheaters, and many in between were rebuilt from one to the other.

The 4-4-0 type was of such balanced proportions as to encourage the application of engineering artistic flare. Many designs emerged which were beautiful to behold, particularly when resplendent in their early liveries. Take, for example, the Midland and LMS 'Compounds', the Great Eastern 'Clauds', the SE&CR 'D' class, the Great North of Scotland 'D40' breed, and the North Eastern 'D20s'. The GW 'Cities' had disappeared by 1948, but there was still elegance to be seen in diverse corners of the system in the form of a few LNW 4-4-0s, the Billinton 'B4X' class, Drummond's 'T9', and the Caledonian 4-4-0s of McIntosh's design.

Of the later 4-6-0s, downgraded to secondary main line work, was any more handsome than the Southern's 'N15X' 'Remembrance' class? Students of the Great Central and North Eastern 4-6-0s would probably answer, 'Yes!'

This splendid and varied collection of classes presented to British Railways just part of a larger nightmare. Variety of equipment to perform similar tasks carries cost penalties. Spares are multiplied, flexibility in operating is reduced, and knowledge of repair methods is often localised in situations such as this. This variety was repeated in other groups of locomotives: freight engines, passenger tanks, shunting tanks and special types all entered BR's stock lists in their multitudes. There were over 400 different classes of steam locomotives in the newly nationalised British Railways; only some of which can be illustrated here. It is small wonder that BR decided to embark on a programme of construction of new standard classes right down to power groups 4, 3 and 2 in an attempt to bring some order out of the chaos which had been bequeathed by history.

The 0-6-0 wheel arrangement had been popular for freight tender engines for over 100 years. These came in many sizes, small-wheeled for heavy goods, and some with wheels as large as 5ft 3in for faster freight. When Reginald Gardiner, in his classic 'Record of Trains' (prewar 78rpm!) said, 'There comes a time in the life of an engine when it becomes long-funnelled and tiresome', surely he had some of these in mind! Would not the Midland '2F' 0-6-0 fit this description?

The LNW 'Cauliflower', Great Eastern 'J15', LSW '0395' class or Caledonian 'Jumbo' were all examples of elderly, long-chimneyed machines which eked out steady existences up rural lines or on minor colliery branches. Most were at the end of their economic life spans, and BR was faced with the dilemma of how to replace them.

Tank engines also exhibited a huge variety in shapes, sizes, wheel arrangements, ages and purposes. Compare the solid girth of a North Eastern 4-8-0T with a puny Midland 0-4-0ST; the elderly grace of a Great Central or North Eastern 4-6-2T with the modern 2-6-4T replacement (LMS or LNER); the 'J94', '57XX', 'USA' dock tank and LMS 'Jinty', all designed for the same shunting arena and all so different! These were eventually replaced by three BR steam designs, plus a surprising variety of diesel shunter types which is a subject in itself!

Probably the best tank engine designs inherited by BR were the latest LMS types, the Fairburn 2-6-4T and the small Class 2 2-6-2T. The 2-6-4Ts came from a long line of steadily developed engines based on the successful Fowler 2-6-4T, improved with Stanier's taper boiler and the modern features of the Fairburn design itself. H. G. Ivatt's 2-6-2T was a very strong little engine with scope for development into quite a potent machine for its size.

The LNER's latest tank engine design, the 'L1' 2-6-4T from Thompson, proved to be technically inferior, achieving low mileages between overhauls. The Great Western 2-6-2Ts were excellent performers but had not been designed for modern conditions with ease of maintenance in mind. Outside valve gear was preferred in the postwar years.

The Southern had few modern tank engines, other than Maunsell's three-cylinder 'Z' class 0-8-0T and 'W' class 2-6-4T freight engines which were 1920s in concept. The acquired 'USA' 0-6-0Ts were modern, simple and indeed excellent for their purpose. They were among the most modern shunting tanks on BR, sharing this distinction with the Hawksworth '15XX' class outside-cylinder pannier tanks on the Western Region. By the end of the 1940s, however, diesel traction had established itself as the means for providing reliable, single-manned shunting power, and further development of steam for this purpose ceased. The Southern's need for modern passenger tank engines arose from that railway's prewar concentration of investment in electrification, which was followed by World War 2 and the consequential lack of investment in locomotives for secondary activities. This led to two very different solutions being evolved and successively delivered early in the days of BR, as discussed in the next chapter.

*Above:*
**British Railways inherited a multitude of 4-4-0 passenger classes. Among the best were the Southern Maunsell rebuilds of SECR Classes D and E, and his later 'L1' class. One of the latter, No 31789, stands at Ashford in September 1956.** *J. M. Jarvis/Colour-Rail BRS223*

*Right:*
**A few early Great Northern 4-4-0s came into BR stock including Class D3 No 2000 (later 62000). Photographed at Grantham just after Nationalisation, it carries decorative green livery specially for its former duties of hauling the LNER directors' saloon.** *J. M. Jarvis/Colour-Rail NE36*

*Above:*
**Fowler produced some of the LMS Class 3 2-6-2Ts with condensing apparatus in an attempt to reduce exhaust emissions in long tunnel sections such as the London Metropolitan 'widened lines'. No 40024 was pictured at Moorgate between duties in 1959, with early LT stock as a background.** *J. G. Dewing/Colour-Rail BRM61*

*Below:*
**No locomotive type has ever run in Britain in larger numbers than the Great Western's Class 57XX 0-6-0 pannier tanks. Recently overhauled at Newton Abbot works, No 5796 had stopped at the top of Torre bank in April 1957 for wagon brakes to be pinned down on the Kingswear goods.** *P. W. Gray/Colour-Rail BRW285*

*Above:*
**The last 2-4-0s in service in Britain were the former Great Eastern 'E4' class. In May 1958 No 62785 pauses at Mildenhall on a branch passenger train.**
*J. G. Dewing/Colour-Rail BRE20*

*Left:*
**BR's smallest passenger tank engines to survive into the 1960s were the GW '14XX' class 0-4-2Ts. Their duties included branch trains such as this one approaching Fowey in Cornwall.**  *Colin Boocock*

*Left:*
**The last examples of the London & South Western Railway locomotive fleet to run on BR were the Adams 'O2' class 0-4-4Ts in the Isle of Wight which were displaced by electrification! Neat little engines they were, like No W18 *Ningwood* which is drifting out of Ventnor tunnel in June 1964 while running round its train prior to departure for Ryde Pier Head.**  *P. Mullett/Colour-Rail BRS314*

*Above:*
**Class 15XX 0-6-0PT No 1508 was photographed at Cardiff Canton in 1961.** *P. J. Hughes/Colour-Rail BRW555*

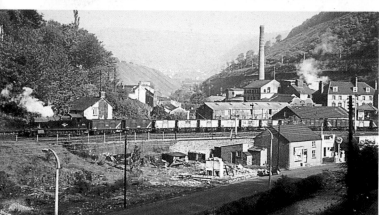

*Left:*
**Welsh valley coal trains ran short distances but needed high tractive effort locomotives. The GWR provided two classes of 2-8-0T and 2-8-2T which were ideal for the task. '5205' class 2-8-0T No 5264 heads a coal train away from Aberbeeg in October 1962.** *W. Potter/Colour-Rail BRW275*

*Left:*
**Some old engines survived their contemporaries in departmental service. One of the LNWR's so-called 'Special Tanks', 0-6-0ST *Earlestown*, is seen shunting at Wolverton carriage works in the 1950s.** *Colour-Rail BRM391*

**In the bleak countryside of the Scottish highlands, ex-Caledonian Railway 0-4-4T No 55217 waits with the branch train at Killin in May 1959.**
*W. J. V. Anderson/Colour-Rail SC133*

# FIVE

# MORE OF THE SAME

While the policy for building standard BR steam locomotive designs was being developed, the need existed in the years from 1948 to 1951 for construction of new locomotives to existing Regional designs.

The London Midland Region went on turning out 'Black 5s' in considerable numbers, including developments with roller bearing axleboxes and manganese steel axlebox and horn liners. Construction also continued of the Ivatt Class 4 2-6-0, his two Class 2 designs (2-6-0 and 2-6-2T) and the Fairburn 2-6-4T.

This new building enabled many of the remaining pre-Grouping designs to be eliminated. The LNWR 'Claughton' and 'Prince of Wales' 4-6-0s at length disappeared, and the last Hughes L&YR 4-6-0 No 50455 was scrapped. The individualistic Scottish companies' few remaining 4-6-0s were quickly eliminated. L&YR 0-8-0s also disappeared and the Midland '3P' 4-4-0s died away. By far the most thorough slaughter however, was the almost total elimination of things LNW: the 'Cauliflowers', 'Coal Tanks' and 'Special Tanks' became memories, and great inroads were made into the ranks of 'G2' 0-8-0s. These engines suffered from light frame construction and were consequently becoming expensive to maintain.

On the Western Region more new 'Castles' appeared, as did further 'Modified Halls', and (more surprisingly, in view of the success of diesel shunters) batches of '94XX' class pannier tanks were constructed, some of which were to see very few years of service indeed.

The WR new construction led quickly to the elimination of many favourite types such as the 'Star' and 'Saint' 4-6-0s, the 'Bulldog' 4-4-0s and 'Dean Goods' 0-6-0s. Odd special classes such as the Midland & South Western Junction 2-4-0s and many South Wales railways' remnants (mainly 0-6-2Ts) disappeared in the early BR years together with the Cambrian 0-6-0s and the last of the GW 0-6-0PTs with open-backed cabs. The Robinson ROD 2-8-0s did not last long into BR, but in this case their demise was in the wake of the arrival of the 'WD' 2-8-0s.

The Eastern and North Eastern Regions continued to turn out 'B1s', 'K1s', 'L1s' and 'A2' Pacifics (the Peppercorn variety). The 'A1' class actually began to emerge in 1948. The most surprising new build on the whole of BR was the decision to turn out from Darlington works a new batch of the North Eastern Railway design 0-6-0T of Class J72. Being a pre-Grouping design, these were thought of as old-fashioned by all who saw them. The need for shunting locomotives in the North-east must have been exceptionally urgent!

New 'B1s' and 'K1s' in their profusion made inroads into pre-Grouping passenger designs on the Eastern and North Eastern systems. All the remaining Great Central 4-6-0s and most of the popular 'Director' 4-4-0s took their leave; Scotland lost its North British 'Scott' class 4-4-0s. The last Great Northern 4-4-0s went, as did most GE 'B12' and 'D16' passenger engines. Smaller machines such as the GE 2-4-0s and 2-4-2Ts did not survive very long into BR, either.

The Southern Region produced the third batch of 'Merchant Navy' class 4-6-2s as well as many light Pacifics during the early BR years. However, the SR's need for new passenger tank engines to replace ancient varieties such as the 'M7' and 'H' 0-4-4Ts and the I1X and I3 4-4-2Ts had not been met. O. V. S. Bulleid had quoted this need in proposing his new general purpose bogie locomotive, the 'Leader' class, the first of which began trials in 1949. Strenuous efforts were made to resolve technical shortcomings but it became clear that the 'Leader' would not be successful. The trials were quickly terminated, and No 36001 and its four partly-completed sisters were scrapped. The BR corporate solution to the SR's tank engine problem was the simple expedient of supplying the Region with the most suitable existing types available elsewhere: the LMS Class 4 2-6-4T and Class 2 2-6-2T. The 2-6-4Ts were built in Brighton works, and settled down well on the Central and Eastern Sections, while the 2-6-2Ts began to make inroads into the 'O2s' and 'M7s'.

The large numbers of new Bulleid 4-6-2s enabled older classes such as most of the Drummond 4-4-0s (other than the 'T9s') and the LBSC 'B4Xs' to be eliminated by displacement, together with 'H1' Atlantics and 'Remembrance' and 'T14' 4-6-0s. Many early 0-6-0 classes were also withdrawn.

The 'LMS engine' solution was also applied to certain areas of the former LNER. Fairburn tanks took over, for example, the Rickmansworth-Aylesbury services. Ivatt Class 4 2-6-0s became common on the M&GN lines, and Class 2 2-6-0s braved the wilds of the Pennines on the routes across from the North-east. The Class 2s even found their way on to the Western Region to displace 'Dean Goods' 0-6-0s. At this point some shortcomings emerged within the 2-6-0s. There was clearly a need to improve this modern breed. A later chapter outlines the excellent improvements BR made to several of the former railways' types, in the interests of more effective and efficient operation.

Mention should perhaps be made at this juncture of the spread of the 733 'WD' 2-8-0s across BR, and of the 25 'WD' 2-10-0s sent to the Scottish Region. Only the Southern needed no 'WDs'. All other Regions found these extremely simple engines competent handlers of freight. The plain looks and ability to run with low maintenance made them appear unlovely and unloved. Their survival to the end of steam on BR was a testimony to their abilities. They were sprightly and strong freight haulage machines capable of matching the performance of the Regional 2-8-0 types. Their high route availability and ease of maintenance made them universally acceptable. In many ways the Riddles 'WD' 2-8-0 might be considered to have been given the role of BR's first Standard design.

**Regional Classes built for British Railways**

*Eastern and North Eastern Regions:*
   'A1' 4-6-2*
   'A2/3' 4-6-2
   'B1' 4-6-0
   'K1' 2-6-0*
   'L1' 2-6-4T
   'J72' 0-6-0T

*London Midland Region:*
   8P 4-6-2
   5 4-6-0
   4 2-6-4T Fairburn
   4 2-6-0 Ivatt
   2 2-6-0 Ivatt
   2 2-6-2T Ivatt

*Southern Region:*
   'Merchant Navy' 4-6-2
   'West Country' 4-6-2†
   'Leader' 0-6-6-0T*

*Western Region:*
   'Castle' 4-6-0
   'Modified Hall' 4-6-0
   'Manor' 4-6-0
   15XX 0-6-0PT*
   16XX 0-6-0PT*
   51XX 2-6-2T
   57XX 0-6-0PT
   74XX 0-6-0PT
   94XX 0-6-0PT

† Includes 'Battle of Britain' class.
* Class introduced after Nationalisation.

NB: Rebuilding continued of 'Royal Scot' 4-6-0s with taper boilers, and of ex-LNWR 'G1' 0-8-0s into 'G2A' class, after Nationalisation.

*Left:*
**The Peppercorn 'A1' class three-cylinder 4-6-2 design emerged in 1949 to swell the East Coast main line fleet. In January 1962 No 60152 *Holyrood* leaves St Boswells on a Waverley route train for Carlisle.**
*D. M. C. Hepburne-Scott/ Colour-Rail SC364*

*Above:*
**The ex-LMS 'Black 5' design was multiplied in the early years of British Railways. One of the BR-built engines, No 44999, leaves Aberdeen with a southbound fish train in 1962.** *D. R. Bissett/Colour-Rail SC356*

*Below:*
**'Castles' continued to emerge from Swindon Works at least until 1950. In June 1962 No 7031 *Cromwell's Castle* leaves Paddington with the 4.45pm to Wolverhampton.** *P. W. Gray/Colour-Rail BRW411*

*Top:*
**Apart from one solitary prototype, all the ER/NER Class K1
2-6-0s were built in BR days. Alnwick is the setting for a
June 1966 departure by No 62011.**
*E. Wilson/Colour-Rail BRE416*

*Above:*
**The Fairburn 2-6-4Ts, such as No 42138 seen here running
round its train at Oxenhope in 1956, were built in large
numbers by BR, some even at Brighton Works for the
Southern Region.** *T. J. Edgington/Colour-Rail BRM307*

*Top:*
**The last 10 Bulleid 'Merchant Navy' Pacifics, plus many of
the light Pacifics, entered service in 1948/49. No 35024** *East
Asiatic Company* **looks superb in the early BR blue livery
when heading a down Weymouth train at Waterloo in June
1949.** *S. C. Townroe/Colour-Rail BRS307*

*Above:*
**BR also built new 'Modified Hall' 4-6-0s. '6959' class 4-6-0
No 7924** *Thornycroft Hall* **passes Twyford with an up
express in the winter of 1959.**
*T. B. Owen/Colour-Rail BRW610*

*Below:*

**Another GWR design of which further examples were built by British Railways was the 'Manor' class. One of these, No 7822 *Foxcote Manor* is seen near Llanbadarn with the morning train to Shrewsbury in December 1958.**
*T. B. Owen/Colour-Rail BRW448*

*Bottom:*

**Some LMS Ivatt Class 2 2-6-0s were built for Western Region routes. One of these, No 46506, is seen with a Moat Lane-Brecon local train near Llanidloes in April 1954.**
*T. B. Owen/Colour-Rail BRW524*

*Above:*
**Painters put the finishing touches to the first Bulleid 'Leader' class 0-6-6-0T No 36001 in Eastleigh Works yard in June 1949. Considerable effort was made to pursue the tests of this engine, but its design problems were not overcome, and the class was prematurely scrapped.**
*S. C. Townroe/Colour-Rail BRS331*

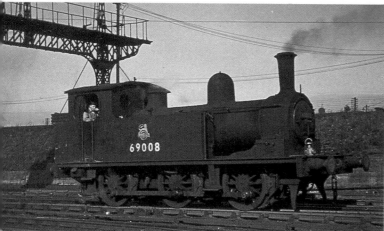

*Left:*
**The North Eastern Railway 0-6-0T design of Class J72 dating from 1898, would hardly seem to be a suitable type of which to build new examples as late as the 1950s, but a batch was constructed by British Railways at Darlington. One of these, No 69008, is seen beneath the gantry at Tyne Dock shed exit in 1951.** *J. Robertson/Colour-rail BRE 414*

*Left:*
**Unliked by enthusiasts who called them 'Doodlebugs' or 'Pigs', the Ivatt Class 4 2-6-0s were in fact very competent engines in their single chimney form. One of the BR-built examples, No 43157, skirts the coast near Caister on Sea in April 1957 with the 3.51pm Yarmouth Beach-Melton Constable on the former MGNJR.**
*E. Alger/Colour-Rail BRE605*

# SIX

# NEW STANDARDS

If a standard range of new steam locomotives was to be produced for BR, several key decisions were doubtless required to be made quickly:

How many different designs were needed to encompass the range of duties?
Should the best existing Regional designs be repeated?
What level of steam technology should be embodied?
To what extent should common components be employed?
How could the new designs balance simplicity with efficiency?
What were the priorities for construction?

The Railway Executive member for mechanical and electrical engineering, R. A. Riddles, had appointed his senior engineers principally from former LMS men. While the aim was to utilise the best practices available, it is not surprising that the LMS influence could be detected throughout the BR Standard locomotive range. Features such as tapered boilers with Belpaire fireboxes, dished smokebox doors, rocking and drop grates, manganese steel axlebox and horn liners, long travel piston valves driven by outside Walschaerts gear, high temperature superheat, high running plates for clear access to moving parts for maintenance and narrowed tender coal spaces for improved backwards view all came from the latest LMS practice.

However, Riddles' desire for the engines to stand out as of BR rather than Regional origin was dealt with by the adoption of a dominant, new exterior design style. This picked out certain common details such as deep valances, enclosed cab layout (new design), chimney tops (actually pure L&YR in shape!), smokebox fronts (GW and Stanier LMS) and smoke deflectors (LNER), to give a family likeness to all engines in the range. The only notable deviations occurred with the smaller locomotives: the Brighton-designed 2-6-4T had curved sides to the tank, cab and bunker, and the Class 3 2-6-2T and both Class 2 types avoided the deep valances to the running plates.

The first engine to appear was the Class 7 Pacific No 70000 *Britannia*. This was a completely new design which bore no direct relationship to any Regional type. The boiler, in size close to a Bulleid 'West Country', had a wide copper firebox. The 6ft 2in coupled wheels could have been either Bulleid or Thompson inspired. The two-cylinder layout was unique among British Pacific classes. At the time (1951) it was announced that this had been made possible by advances in balancing theory since the former railways' 4-6-2s had been designed. In fact, the Germans had operated bigger two-cylinder 4-6-2s in express services since 1925.

Observers were surprised that only a single blast pipe and chimney were provided on No 70000. In reality, this produced sufficient draught for an engine designed to be worked with full regulator and not-too-short cut-off settings. Drivers coped with this feature with different results. There was no problem on the GE lines where hard-pressing of locomotives was not unusual; on the WR many could not come to terms with the different handling required. Generally, the 'Britannias' could perform brilliantly and economically, and fully justified their batch production straight off the drawing board. Crews appreciated the enclosed cabs and well-placed controls, though SR drivers regretted the absence of electric lighting. The GE batch revolutionised train speeds on the Norwich and Cambridge main lines.

More controversy surrounded the Class 6 'Clan' 4-6-2 when that appeared. Basically a 'Britannia' with a smaller boiler, its introduction was presumably to meet a need for power on lines of lower route availability. They were deployed on the Glasgow & South Western routes and on the northern end of the West Coast main line. No more than 10 were built and hindsight indicates they found no unique role to fill.

The Class 5 4-6-0, on the other hand, had the potential to be built in large numbers. Its boiler was clearly based on the LMS Class 5. The engine used the same 6ft 2in wheels as did the Standard Pacifics, and its valve gear, also like the 4-6-2s, was clearly Doncaster inspired. The result was an excellent machine, capable of being flogged without steaming difficulties, and able to run fast when required. It was also at home on fitted freight work. The Standard 5's performance edge over the LMS 'Black 5', the 'B1' and 'Hall' was not so significant as to dampen Regional preferences for their own designs, except on the Southern where they beat the 'King Arthurs' on their own ground, and on the Somerset & Dorset where they remained the firm favourites from their introduction to the closure of that line. A group of engines was also supplied with Caprotti valve gear, towards the end of the class deliveries. Operationally, the Standard Class 5s worked predominantly on the Scottish, Southern and London Midland Regions.

Next down the scale came the three Class 4 designs. No 80010 was the first 2-6-4T to be delivered. Essentially a tidied-up Fairburn 2-6-4T, these machines were built in relatively large numbers for all Regions except the Western (whose Prairie tanks ruled the roost until dieselisation). The Class 4 4-6-0 was a strange beast, virtually a Class 5 with smaller boiler, cylinders and 5ft 8in wheels. It was in the operating range of the WR 'Manor' 4-6-0 but had no other real Regional equivalent. The Class 4 4-6-0s went principally to the Western, London Midland and Southern Regions. They worked capably but rarely exceptionally. There was also the Class 4 2-6-0, clearly based on the Ivatt Class 4 2-6-0 in all principal dimensions but with a big improvement in looks. These worked very well indeed on Southern, Eastern, North Eastern and LM Region secondary services, though they tended to become mechanically quite rough at high mileages.

One can with hindsight regret that the obvious derivative was not built. A 2-6-0 version of the 5ft 8in 2-6-4T would have been a winner in performance and general flexibility, as versatile as the former NCC 2-6-0 type in Northern Ireland. It might have equalled the 4-6-0's performance, bettered the 5ft 3in 2-6-0, and reduced the variety of boiler designs by one, had it been substituted for the other two designs.

The Class 3 2-6-0 was a Class 4 2-6-0 with a smaller boiler, not as small as the Ivatt Class 2 boiler, but reportedly based on that of a GW Prairie. This was another class not built in large numbers. One wonders in retrospect whether the gap between the Class 4 and Class 2 was really worth bridging. It had a 2-6-2T derivative, used quite widely on SR and WR branches, but they were occasionally quite competently deputised for by Class 2s. The Class 3 2-6-2T was a handsome tank engine, certainly, and sufficiently liked on the Western to receive green livery in later years.

The smallest standard designs were the Class 2 2-6-0 and 2-6-2T, basically Ivatt engines without top feeds and with minor detail differences only. Indeed, most parts were common with the LMS engines, even though their drawing numbers were changed to BR ones, thus disguising their LMS origins! Both classes were good performers. The 2-6-2Ts were fitted with vacuum push-pull control apparatus. In this form a few were transferred to replace push-pull fitted 'M7s', only to find that the SR push-pull system used compressed air to operate the regulator remotely! The push-pull gear was removed by the SR at Eastleigh works.

Then came the '9Fs'. These 2-10-0s were the only BR Standard design that met an operating need that could not have been covered by a Regional type. Col H. C. B. Rogers' book *Riddles and the '9Fs'* (Ian

Allan) describes their design and history succinctly. They were clearly quite excellent engines. The boiler was slightly smaller than the Class 7, redesigned so as to pitch the wide firebox over 5ft 0in coupled wheels, a feat never previously achieved within the British loading gauge. The 10-coupled wheelbase embodied the curving flexibility which Riddles had used on his 'WD' 2-10-0s, and the use of minimal rotating balancing produced an engine capable of a surprising turn of speed.

The '9Fs' were ideal for the heavy, fitted freight regime which was spreading across British Railways. They handled block oil trains with as much ease as heavy coal trains, and came, almost too late, to be the only locomotive able to take 12-coach passenger trains over the Mendips without a pilot locomotive. Indeed, the fact that they could run at up to 90mph with 5ft 0in, 10-coupled wheels put them onto main line expresses on occasions as deputies for Pacifics!

Ten '9Fs' were built with Crosti feed water heating drums under a slightly smaller boiler design than the standard '9Fs'. The aim was to achieve an efficiency improvement to match that claimed for Italian locomotives so fitted. It is, however, always difficult to improve on the excellent. While thermal efficiency did improve, increased maintenance costs were caused by corrosion in the preheater drums. The drums were subsequently removed and the locomotives converted to a normal layout. They retained their smaller boilers, however, and their odd looks.

The '9F' 2-10-0 No 92220 *Evening Star* was BR's last new steam locomotive, but the '9F' class was not the last new steam class to be introduced to BR. While other types were under construction, No 71000 *Duke of Gloucester* emerged as the prototype Class 8P 4-6-2. Not as large as an LMS or LNER 8P Pacific, No 71000's development period was brief and the design was not put into series production. It used a Class 7 boiler barrel with a longer firebox, over a three-cylinder layout using Caprotti poppet valve gear for effective steam distribution. Why its maximum theoretical output was not achieved may yet be revealed, operating in preservation, following modifications to the ashpan and draughting.

We are now blessed with hindsight, through which we can form views on the variety of Standard classes actually produced. Clearly, the close spacing of 11 of the 12 designs enabled any engine to deputise for one in the next higher power class. Such operating flexibility was used, certainly. But the principle was not followed on the Southern, and not always either on overseas systems. An alternative would be to build fewer types at wider power spacings, ensuring that sufficient number were built at the 'big engine' end of the spectrum. Had this policy been adopted, the BR designs could have been reduced to the number of classes shown in the accompanying table, assuming the appearance of a 2-6-0 tender version of the 2-6-4T.

There could then have been eight instead of 12 locomotive types, and six instead of 10 boiler designs.

**BR Standard Steam Classes — an Alternative Range**

| Power Class | Type | Wheel diameter | Boiler size |
|---|---|---|---|
| '9F' | 2-10-0 | 5ft 0in | 9F |
| '8P' | 4-6-2 | 6ft 2in | 8P |
| '7MT' | 4-6-2 | 6ft 2in | 7 |
| '5MT' | 4-6-0 | 6ft 2in | 5 |
| '4MT' | 2-6-0 | 5ft 8in | 4 |
| '4MT' | 2-6-4T | 5ft 8in | 4 |
| '2MT' | 2-6-0 | 5ft 0in | 2 |
| '2MT' | 2-6-2T | 5ft 0in | 2 |

A list of classes actually built is near the end of Appendix 1.

It is probably churlish to make such suggestions, because the Standard range provided BR with an effective and economical fleet of steam locomotives which could have held the fort competently until the advent of widespread main line electrification. The change in policy towards rapid dieselisation and the rationalisation of the BR system, which together caused the Standard locomotives to have such short lives, were no reflection on the locomotives themselves.

It was an odd quirk of fate, was it not, which resulted in building ceasing when the BR Standard locomotive fleet had reached just one short of its first thousand?

**The good looks of the 'Britannias' matched their spritely performance on the Great Eastern main line services. No 70003 *John Bunyan* is portrayed at Thetford in March 1962.** *J. J. Davis/Colour-Rail BRE248*

The '9F' 2-10-0 design filled an urgent need for heavy freight power most effectively. No 92064 is pictured at Stanley with coal for Consett. *J. G. Dewing/Colour-Rail BRE609*

The free running '9F' 2-10-0s were ideal for passenger trains on the heavily graded Somerset & Dorset line. The 9.53am from Bath to Bournemouth West passes a trackside garden at Midsomer Norton in August 1962 with No 92001 at the head.  *P. Mullett/Colour-Rail SD67*

*Above:*

**Only 10 'Clans' were built and they spent most of their lives on West Coast services north of Preston, and on the Glasgow & South Western lines. In June 1961 No 72003 *Clan Fraser* heads a Liverpool-Glasgow train near Greenholm.** *Derek Cross/Colour-Rail BRM325*

*Below:*

**One of the competent BR Class 5 4-6-0s, No 73015, climbs the Lickey incline with a northbound passenger working in 1956.** *W. A. Thompson/Colour-Rail BRM518*

*Top:*
**Another Standard Class 5 photographed in 1963 brings a freight through Nottingham Victoria station.**
*Don Beecroft/Colour-Rail BRE603*

*Above:*
**The Standard Class 4 2-6-0, represented here by No 76017 photographed after overhaul at Eastleigh, was a neat design and a lively performer.**   *Colin Boocock*

*Left:*
**The medium size Class 3 2-6-0 was in effect a Class 4 with a smaller boiler. In Scotland in March 1961, No 77015 crosses Glenbuck Loch causeway with a Muirkirk local.**
*Derek Cross/Colour-Rail SC89*

Class 3 2-6-2T No 82020 stands at Machynlleth shed in September 1962, carrying unlined green livery.
*J. G. Dewing/Colour-Rail BRW31*

On the Western Region's Cambrian line near Carno, Standard Class 2 2-6-0 No 78003 makes a charming picture as it hauls a short school train in September 1962.
*J. G. Dewing/Colour-Rail BRW33*

*Right:*
**The well-balanced lines of the BR Class 4MT Standard 2-6-4T design are displayed by No 80153, seen at Eastleigh depot in April 1957, just outshopped from an Intermediate overhaul.** *Colin Boocock*

*Below:*
**The solitary '8P' Pacific No 71000 *Duke of Gloucester* poses at Camden depot.** *J. G. Dewing/Colour-Rail BRM12*

*Left:*
**Class 2 2-6-2T No 84014 crosses Park Bridge on the Oldham Clegg Street line in 1965.** *B. Magilton/Colour-Rail BRE520*

# SEVEN

# IMPROVING THE BREED

The early postwar years were not a time of plenty, as many had supposed they would be. Six years of national economic activity had been diverted towards defeating Hitler's Naziism on the European continent, and in stemming the tide of Japanese imperialism in the Far East. For many years afterwards the armed forces retained large numbers of manpower. The years of civil and industrial reconstruction which followed the war were marked by various shortages, including manpower and fuel. Such were not ideal conditions for running a fleet of ageing steam locomotives in an era when public expectations were high. In Britain there were intense demands to raise train speeds to prewar levels, yet the 1930s-type availability of good steam coal and relatively cheap manpower were not likely to be repeated.

Consequently, there was a need to improve on many of the older express steam locomotive types which had been designed for more ideal operating conditions than obtained in BR days. Quite a number of the newer designs which had appeared in more recent years also required improvement in the light of early experience.

The coal quality situation affected locomotives designed for specific types of coal. Those of the Great Western Railway, for example, steamed best on good Welsh steam coal. That railway had blessed its vast locomotive works at Swindon with a locomotive testing plant on which engines could be run on rollers linked to dynamometers which could absorb and record the output from the locomotive. This enabled a locomotive to be tested in controlled conditions statically, which in turn facilitated the measurement of performance indicators such as cylinder and exhaust pressures, blast pipe pressure, superheater steam temperatures, and smokebox vacuum. British Railways also commissioned a more modern test plant at Rugby which was able to handle the largest Pacific locomotives. The Rugby plant carried out a number of detailed tests on principal classes, and the published test reports proved valuable in making comparisons as well as enabling potential improvements to be pinpointed.

Both test plants were in the charge of teams of engineers able to analyse test results and to derive from the findings intelligent solutions to problems. In many ways, the Swindon team could probably claim the greater success rate, because most significant and simple solutions to locomotive steaming problems emerged as a result of their work.

Thus it was that, after more than 25 years of operating 'Kings' and 'Castles' with relatively low superheat, these locomotives were brought into line with those of the other Regions and were fitted with high temperature superheat. The experiments with draughting on the Swindon test plant resulted in all the 'Kings' being fitted with double blastpipes and chimneys, which gave their performance on the road a new lease of life, and fortunately did not diminish their stylish appearance. The 'Castles' had always been good performers in their class, and, as was to happen with other classes subsequently, it proved less easy to improve upon a winner. The fitting of double chimneys to 'Castles' (like Bulleid's fitting of Lemaître exhausts to SR 'Schools') was not pursued beyond a relatively small number. On the other hand, the relatively modern 'County' class 4-6-0 did find benefit, and all were fitted with double chimneys, in this case a squat variety that was shorter than the other boiler mountings.

As mentioned in the chapter on new building of Regional types, the LMS Ivatt Class 2 2-6-0 design which had been brought onto Welsh border routes to displace 'Dean Goods' 0-6-0s was being criticised by train crews, so one of the 2-6-0s was put on the Swindon test rollers. It was found that the Derby design had too wide a chimney to enable adequate draughting of the fire for good steam production. Following fitting of a correctly proportioned chimney, the resulting improvement brought the boiler up to an excellent standard of steaming that matched the undoubted strength of the engine. All subsequent builds of this class and its mate, the Class 2 2-6-2T, incorporated the narrow internal chimney dimensions, though the later ones had a double-walled chimney casting which enabled a more aesthetically satisfactory external chimney profile to be achieved.

The other Ivatt 2-6-0 design, his Class 4, had been fitted from new with a double blastpipe and chimney. This engine, in contrast to most others needing modification, was over-draughted in this form; the ability to draw unburned fuel from the fire and throw it out of the chimney does not lead to economy, however well the boiler steams! In this case the solution was a single blastpipe and chimney, which as a compensation also much improved the locomotive's appearance. Nevertheless, these engines laboured under disagreeable nicknames varying from 'Doodlebugs' to 'Pigs' throughout their useful lives.

It was on the LNER big engine fleet that some of the most startling progress was made. Sir Nigel Gresley had already fitted double Kylchap exhausts to some 'A4s' before the war, and *Mallard's* 126mph bore testimony to the free running which that device encouraged. Not only did it raise the draught available for the fire, it also reduced the back-pressure at the blastpipe. Quite logically, therefore, all the 'A4s' received this device, as did all the Thompson and Peppercorn Pacifics from new.

British Railways was able to develop this theme further with the 'V2' 2-6-2s and the old 'A3' class 4-6-2s. On these classes new cylinders were provided, the outward, visible sign being straight, outside steam pipes to the outside cylinders. Double Kylchaps were fitted, and the transformation was almost complete. The 'A3' class performance reached levels in normal traffic that had rarely been surpassed in prewar years, so good was the improvement achieved. One snag was the drifting of steam to obscure the driver's view, resulting from the lower exhaust pressure. Uniquely in British practice, the 'A3s' were fitted with German style 'blinker' smoke deflector plates either side of the smokebox. Controversial though this undoubtedly was in the eyes of the many who loved the classic Great Northern lines of these lovely engines, it did bring to their appearance a modern image which matched their excellent performance!

In the case of the Bulleid Pacifics, there were problems a-many to resolve. The cut-off drift at speed due to the valve gear characteristics has already been mentioned, as have their high maintenance costs and relatively low reliability, though they were becoming more dependable as detail difficulties were systematically resolved by the engineers. The draughting of the boilers and the free running of the engines were never in doubt. Therefore the process of rebuilding these locomotives was begun. The Bulleid valve gear gave way to three independent sets of Walschaerts, curing at a stroke the cut-off and overrun problems. Steam reverse was replaced by an accurate manual screw reverse so that control was secure. The steam control to the firehole door was removed in the interests of simplicity. The plate 'dustbin' chimney and petticoat were replaced by properly shaped castings and a new ashpan was fitted; both were changes which improved the completeness of combustion. Manganese steel axlebox and horn liners were fitted, to extend the period between overhauls. Frame stretchers were strengthened, and the coupled wheels rebalanced. A cylindrical smokebox was riveted flush with the front ring of the boiler barrel. The air-smoothed casing gave way to conventional exterior 'furniture' designed to bring the Pacifics' appearance close to the BR Standard family looks.

The rebuilt Bulleid Pacifics were totally successful. At around £8,500 each the work was expensive. A back check was carried out on savings actually achieved from better coal consumption and lower maintenance and overhaul costs. This proved that the rebuilding work had paid for itself. As for the myth that free running had been impaired by the change in valve gear, top speeds of the rebuilt 'Merchant Navy' locomotives were recorded above 100mph, just as before rebuilding. All 30 'MNs' and 60 of the 110 light Pacifics were rebuilt, before the work ceased in the light of the realisation that steam's life expectancy was now short.

Of the BR Standard designs, only one appeared to need improvement. The Class 4 4-6-0 met most of the needs of its power class, but was lacking in reserve when called upon to deputise for bigger Class 5 locomotives. Some Class 4 4-6-0s were fitted with double chimneys and blastpipes, which rectified this problem, an interesting contrast to what befell the LMS Ivatt Class 4 2-6-0s!

Nevertheless the desire to tinker is always there, and one '9F' was fitted with a Giesl ejector chimney, as was one unrebuilt 'Battle of Britain' Pacific. In neither case did the device produce more than a marginal improvement, illustrating how well the steam circuits and draughting of modern steam engines had been developed. (The Giesl ejector had worked very well on older, less efficient engines overseas.)

One can conclude that BR's steam locomotive policy was broad and positive in outlook. Not only were good, modern standard designs produced, they were backed by intelligently improved older locomotives. Towards the end of steam, there were very few 'duds', if any, in BR's locomotive stud.

*Left:*
The rebuilding of the Stanier 'Turbomotive' turbine 4-6-2 produced this splendidly handsome engine, reminiscent of a cross between a 'Princess Royal' and a 'Duchess'. No 46202 was unhappily destroyed in the Harrow & Wealdstone accident in 1952.   *W. H. Foster/Colour-Rail BRM789*

*Below:*
Double blastpipes and chimneys together with higher temperature superheat put new life into the ex-GWR 'King' class 4-6-0s. No 6019 *King Henry V* scatters the contents of the water troughs at Goring as it speeds towards Paddington with the up 'Red Dragon' in March 1961.
*T. B. Owen/Colour-Rail BRW389*

*Above:*
**The double chimney on 'County' class 4-6-0 No 1007 *County of Brecknock* had a squat appearance. The locomotive was photographed in August 1959 leaving Saltash with the 'Cornish Riviera Limited'** *T. B. Owen/Colour-Rail BRW602*

*Left:*
**A rejuvenated 'A3' 4-6-2 with double Kylchap exhaust, No 60103 *Flying Scotsman*, heads the down 'Yorkshire Pullman' in August 1960 near Hadley Wood.**
*J. F. Aylard/Colour-Rail BRE90*

*Left:*
**The Southern attempted to curb the spark throwing of the Lemaitre five-jet blast pipe by replacing it on No 35019 *French Line CGT* with a single blastpipe and chimney. This 'Merchant Navy' was thus noisier to the ear, and in this form it is seen passing Shawford in the winter of 1954.**
*B. J. Swain/Colour-Rail BRS376*

*Above:*

**Fitting a double chimney and blastpipe to the Standard 4 4-6-0s such as No 75029, seen here in 1966 at Machynlleth, enabled these locomotives to steam better when working at the upper end of their power range.**

*J. R. Besley/Colour-Rail BRW571*

*Below:*

**No 35024 *East Asiatic Company* exhibits the handsome lines of the rebuilt 'Merchant Navy' class as it pauses at Southampton Central.**

*G. W. Parry collection/Colour-Rail BRS472*

*Left:*
**Bulleid Pacifics of both groups were rebuilt to improve their maintenance and fuel costs. The train engine of this Manchester-Bournemouth relief to the down 'Pines Express' is rebuilt 'West Country' No 34040 *Crewkerne*. 4-6-0 No 75027 provides head end assistance for the Mendip inclines. The photograph was taken at Midford on the Somerset & Dorset line in 1962.** *W. Potter/Colour-Rail SD142*

*Left:*
**Some Maunsell 'N' and 'U' class 2-6-0s were improved by being given new cylinders and BR Standard design chimneys. 'N' 2-6-0 No 31853 sported these modifications in August 1960 when working a Padstow train near Halwill.** *Don Beecroft/Colour Rail BRS474*

*Below:*
**Ugly is as ugly does! The 10 Crosti '9F' 2-10-0s were not an improvement on the standard '9F' design because severe corrosion within the pre-heating barrel caused excessive maintenance costs. No 92028 was seen at Finedon Road in July 1959.** *K. C. H. Fairey/Colour-Rail BRM615*

# EIGHT

# HOMES AND HOSPITALS

Along with its 20,000 steam locomotives, British Railways inherited an infrastructure of about 350 depots to which the locomotives were allocated for maintenance, and 21 locomotive works capable of undertaking periodic overhauls.

It sometimes comes as a surprise to be reminded how much attention steam locomotives required. As an example of the most basic work necessary to keep an old engine running, one can recall that on arrival at Ventnor on the Isle of Wight, after less than 20 miles of a return trip to Ryde Pier Head, it was necessary for the fireman to open the smokebox door and shovel from the smokebox volumes of ash which had collected around the foot of the blastpipe just behind the door. To save time this was done while the 'O2' 0-4-4T took water. Modern types of engine were fitted with deflector plates within the smokebox which were designed to direct the draught to pick up loose deposits and fling them up the chimney. This so-called 'self-cleaning' smokebox was one device designed to reduce the labour content of steam operation.

Basic attention needed at least once every working day included coaling. Whilst locomotive water tanks could be and were replenished at stations, yards or loops en route, filling of bunkers or tenders with coal required a visit to a depot, or at least one of the small sub-depots at strategic locations. Coaling methods varied substantially. Major depots often had high, concrete coaling plants, capable of hopper discharge straight into a tender or bunker. These plants were usually fed by lifting a coal wagon on a hoist up the side of the tower, and tippling it at the top so that its contents fell into the large hopper below. Use of such plants was relatively efficient in labour, but had the disadvantage of preventing special selection of good coal for locomotives of specific types or for special duties. All engines thus received the same, broken up mixture. Coaling plants like this were common on the LMS and LNER, and the SR had one at Nine Elms and another at Exmouth Junction.

Other depots delivered coal to locomotives by means of skips. Usually there was an inclined ramp up which an aged, small tank engine would push coal wagons which were then unloaded by shovel into individual skips. When a locomotive arrived for coaling, several skips were discharged by tipping their contents into a chute which fed the coal into the tender. Other staff standing on the tender would distribute the coal into the most effective stack shape. This was quite a labour-intensive method, but it was a very common one. All railways used variations of this type of coal stage, even the Great Western at its largest depot, Old Oak Common.

Yet another coaling method used a swing jib crane. Again, wagons in a nearby siding were emptied by shovel into skips. Each was lifted by crane to the tender being filled. Usually by pulling a lever at the back of the skip, a man would open its bottom door and the coal would cascade into the area required. At least this method ensured better placement of the coal in the tender, but it was a slow business to load five or six tons, and also was labour intensive. It was distinctly unpleasant in cold or wet weather!

Discharging ash from the ashpan at the end of a diagram's work was another regular and time-consuming task. Modern locomotives had rocking and drop grates to enable ash and clinker to be more easily broken up and then dropped from the firebox into the ashpan. Nonetheless, rodding out an ashpan to ensure all ash was dropped into a pit was a singularly unpleasant task. Usually another man had to come along later, often with a shovel and wheelbarrow, to dig out the ash from the pit and transfer it to a wagon for final disposal. Ash was used widely in the formation of depot yard surfaces and footpaths, but beware the unwary from treading on ash floating over a flooded manhole or hydrant!

To prevent boilers from scaling up it was necessary to wash out the water passages therein, particularly those around the firebox. This was sensibly achieved when the boiler had cooled. Washout plugs were removed and water hoses were applied through each plug in turn, until the discharge from the lowest plugs was clean.

While ashpans, fireboxes, smokeboxes, coal bunkers and water tanks needed frequent attention, steam locomotives required basic maintenance at intervals from a few days to several weeks. The maintenance of steam locomotives was the responsibility of the depots to which they were allocated. Mechanical maintenance was usually under a specialist mechanical foreman. His gangs of fitters and mates tackled almost anything, other than boiler repairs, the boilermakers' job. Repairs to engines varied widely from replacing leaking steam glands, through renewing worn brake blocks and cleaning out injectors to get them going again, to the really heavy work of lifting an engine to remove axleboxes for remetalling. To ensure that no impending problem was overlooked, the locomotives underwent a series of inspections at regular intervals of days, weeks and months. The really skilled work included ensuring that piston valves or slide valves were properly set so that steam input to, and exhaust from, the cylinders were timed correctly.

Inside a large engine shed were, typically, parallel tracks with shallow pits between the rails. Usually one or two tracks were designated as washout roads, and others were either for stabling, preparation or repairs. Principal depots usually had a small bay or separate shop with lifting equipment: a sheerlegs hoist, jacks or, in extremely well equipped cases such as Old Oak Common, a heavy overhead crane. Sometimes this was backed by a small group of machine tools such as lathes, a shaper and a boring machine.

The larger motive power depots also stabled and looked after a breakdown train. These consisted generally of a stores and packing van, a staff vehicle and a 30- or 45-ton steam breakdown crane. When a derailment occurred (in the days of many small, loose-coupled wagons derailments were frequent, particularly in marshalling yards) the extraction of men from the depot to man the breakdown train often left only a skeleton staff to continue maintenance or repair of the engines there.

One of the more psychologically rewarding activities at a steam depot was engine cleaning, the starting grade in the footplate line of promotion. Locomotives got cleaned if they were able to be stopped on days (young people were barred from shift working), if they could be spared from train running, and if there were sufficient cleaning staff available. Otherwise things just became dirtier! Normally a priority system emerged at a depot, the top link passenger engines getting adequate cleaning while freight and yard pilots were often left uncleaned.

After about 50,000-90,000 miles of running, the axleboxes and horns of a steam locomotive became slack, piston rings often wore and let steam by, frame stretchers and motion brackets began to work loose and in some cases cracks began to appear in the main frames. Sorting out these problems presented a volume and standard of work beyond the capability of depots.

The main works to which engines were sent for overhaul were dominated by high, long erecting shops, surrounded by other shops undertaking boiler and tender repairs and component repair and manufacture. There were machine shops, fitting shops, forges, smithies and foundries. Shops specialised in wheels, brasswork, tool repairs and patternmaking. The works were supported by large stores, amenity blocks including canteens, production offices and management and accountancy sections. The main shops were noisy hives of activity, and totally fascinating to a visitor from the world outside.

At an intermediate overhaul, a locomotive would be pushed into the erecting shop, separated from its tender and moved by overhead cranes to a stripping bay. Here its rods and valve gear were dismantled and its brakework, cab and boiler fittings removed. Two overhead cranes, usually of 50-60 tons capacity each and supported on runways at eaves level along the shop, picked up the locomotive (still carrying its boiler) leaving its wheels and axleboxes behind, and trundled off down the shop with it, slewing it to one side so as to lower it carefully onto prepared stands. Here, during the next week and a few days, it received overhauled injectors, cab and boiler fittings. Any fractures were welded up, loose bolts tightened, horn liners replaced or adjusted for clearance and the frames were cleaned. Paintwork was usually touched up. If cylinders needed reboring, this was done using a rig clamped to the cylinder.

Meanwhile, the wheels had gone off to the wheel shop to have their tyres turned or replaced by new. Bearing surfaces needing attention were skimmed and polished, as were the bosses for coupling and connecting rods. Coupled wheels from high speed engines were placed in a balancing machine and spun, to check and correct any tendency to imbalance following repair. Lead was either added to or removed from the balance weight pockets in the wheels. Axleboxes requiring remetalling were turned upside down, and molten white metal poured into a mould clamped to the box. The axleboxes were then trucked to the machine shop for the rough cast white metal to be machined to a smooth surface, and the oil channels cut in.

Other components such as coupling and connecting rods and valve gear, brake cylinders and rodding, and piston valves, went to a fitting shop for new or remetalled bushes, and new piston rings to be fitted.

Eventually, the repaired bits and pieces came back together in the erecting shop and the locomotive was reassembled, the major operation of lowering down onto the wheels (and later the bogies) being carried out with care and precision. The engine was then lifted onto small rollers to enable the coupled wheels to be levered round to facilitate valve setting.

Once shunted out of the erecting shop, a short run light in steam was a common practice, to ensure all bearings and bushes were free from binding and that any steam leaks were noted and eliminated.

When the second or third major overhaul in a sequence was due, often after about five years of running, a steam locomotive received a general overhaul. The principal difference from the intermediate overhaul described before was that the boiler was removed from the frames, stripped of its lagging and mountings, and given a very thorough inspection and overhaul. Repairs arising from the inspection normally included some re-staying and retubing, and recaulking of joints or stay heads. They frequently went as far as cutting out and welding in, or riveting on, patches to replace wasted areas, or even fitting a complete new firebox or tubeplate. When repairs to a boiler were complete, it would be taken to a stand outside the shop, its openings fitted with blanking plates, and the boiler subjected to hydraulic pressure to a level more than double its maximum working pressure. Water hydraulic testing was the safest method because leaks would be immediately visible and if disaster should unluckily strike, no explosion could result. After any repairs had been carried out, a fire would be lit under the firebox, and the boiler subjected to a steam test to a higher pressure than the working pressure. Only after repairs arising from that test had been completed and proven, was the boiler considered ready to be returned to the erecting shop for placement on a locomotive's frames.

Towards the end of a general repair the complete locomotive was repainted, then taken outside and given a static steam test before its trial run. On return to its home depot, this gleaming apparition would soon gather a thin film of workaday dirt, and only weeks later would be scarcely distinguishable from its colleagues!

## Locomotive Works in 1948

*Eastern Region:*
  Doncaster*
  Stratford
  Gorton

*London Midland Region:*
  Derby*
  Crewe*
  Horwich*
  Bow

*North Eastern Region:*
  Darlington*

*Scottish Region:*
  Saint Rollox
  Cowlairs
  Inverurie
  Loch Gorm

*Southern Region:*
  Eastleigh*
  Ashford
  Brighton*
  Ryde (IoW)

*Western Region:*
  Swindon*
  Wolverhampton
  Caerphilly
  Newton Abbot
  Oswestry

*Works still undertaking new building of steam traction as well as overhauls.

**The heaviest work on steam locomotives was undertaken at the main workshops such as Eastleigh, where a newly rebuilt 'West Country' 4-6-2 is seen being lowered on to its wheels.** *Colin Boocock*

*Above:*
**A new Class 9F 2-10-0 is under construction in the great erecting shop at Swindon. This works produced the last new steam locomotive for BR in 1960.** *Colin Boocock*

*Below:*
**The vastness of the Swindon Works 'A Shop' displays locomotives Nos 75003, 1029, 6029, 7015 and 70027, and many others. A traverser ran the length of the shop enabling locomotives to be placed into each bay.**
*T. B. Owen/Colour-Rail BRW685*

*Left:*
At major cities to which ran more than one of the pre-Grouping railways, even in BR days there was often a separate locomotive depot for each former railway's stock. Bristol was no exception, where the former LMS depot was this one, at Barrow Road, where GW visitors were lately common. *P. W. Gray/Colour-Rail BRM771*

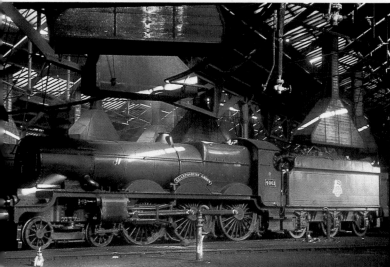

*Left:*
Former Great Western Railway 'Star' class 4-6-0, No 4061 *Glastonbury Abbey* stands on the turntable in one of the Old Oak Common roundhouses in September 1955. *T. B. Owen/Colour-Rail BRW414*

*Below:*
The Great Western preferred roundhouses for its major depots, such as this view of engines around one of the turntables in Swindon depot. Included in the picture are Nos 2244, 9773, 4178 and 9605. *A. E. Doyle/Colour-Rail BRW386*

*Above:*
**A large depot could often display a huge variety of steam locomotives. This was the scene at Eastleigh shed yard in the untypical days of the 1955 ASLEF strike.**
*S. C. Townroe/Colour-Rail BRS336*

*Left:*
**Home for the Killin branch engine was this small shed at Loch Tay. This scene shows Caledonian 0-4-4T No 55217 being prepared for a day's branch line service in April 1961.** *D. M. C. Hepburne-Scott/Colour-Rail SC344*

*Top right:*
**Under the coaling plant at Perth motive power depot in 1959 stands red 'Coronation' Pacific No 46247 *City of Liverpool*.**
*W. J. V. Anderson/Colour-Rail SC120*

*Bottom right:*
**Seven locomotives are grouped around the turntable in Ebbw Junction roundhouse in September 1963.**
*T. B. Owen/Colour-Rail BRW534*

**Barrow Road shed yard is crowded as locomotives await attention one evening in 1961.**
*T. B. Owen/Colour-Rail BRM549*

**Nos 45592 Indore and 46148 The Manchester Regiment pose outside Camden depot, London, in 1962.**
*J. G. Dewing/Colour-Rail BRM772*

*Above:*
**This LMS line-up in 1958 at Kentish Town shed comprises Class 5 No 44822, '4F' 0-6-0 No 44563, '2P' 4-4-0 No 40413 and 'Jubilee' No 45724 *Warspite*.**
*T. B. Owen/Colour-Rail BRM551*

*Left:*
**One of the many medium sized depots in the industrial north was Barnsley, seen in August 1959.**
*G. Warnes/Colour-Rail BRE521*

*Left:*
**In 1961 it was possible to see 'A3s' with German-style smoke deflectors in large numbers. Two of them, Nos 60062 *Minoru* and 60039 *Sandwich*, flank engines Nos 60025 *Falcon*, 60906, and 60028 *Walter K. Whigham* at King's Cross 'Top Shed'.** *P. Mullett/Colour-Rail BRE320*

# NINE

# STEAM'S LAST STAND

Two events combined to accelerate the decline and fall of the steam locomotive on British Railways. Firstly, there was the political support for the speeding up of diesel locomotive and multiple-unit deliveries in the late 1950s. Secondly, when the route rationalisations following the Beeching reports made their impact in the mid-1960s, the number of locomotives required for traffic on BR fell very rapidly. Consequently, the latest steam locomotives built had very short lives. The first BR Standard locomotive was delivered in 1951, the last in 1960. All had gone by late 1968, and no BR Standard engine lasted more than 17 years. Many saw as little as seven years' active service.

When sufficient diesels had been delivered to make an impact on the principal routes, there developed a policy of blanket dieselisation of certain large areas. Thus the Liverpool Street division of the Eastern Region became the first on BR to be fully cleared of steam operation, other than of services penetrating into it. The Western was the first Region to lose its allocated steam locomotives. In no way did the choices reflect the quality or age of the engines there. It was the nature and direction of the spread of modern traction which caused the former Great Western types to be the first pre-Nationalisation engines to be eliminated from the rails of BR. This occurred in the winter of 1964/65.

In the other Regions, the few remaining pre-Grouping classes disappeared first, with the notable exception of the North Eastern Railway 'Q6' and 'J27' locomotives. These survived as late as 1966 on their home ground in Tees and Tyneside, probably a full four years beyond most other pre-1923 classes, of which a few ex-LBSCR 0-6-2Ts were among the last to go in the SR's purge of 1962.

What certainly did not happen, as many had supposed would be the case, was the expected survival of BR Standard designs beyond all the Regional types. In almost every area that lost its steam traction, Regional classes were prominent among the last survivors. This was not surprising on the Western where BR types had scarcely become popular, nor on the East Coast main line where Gresley, Thompson and Peppercorn Pacifics kept all the top jobs until ousted by the 'Deltics' and other diesel-electrics. But on the Southern's South Eastern division, for example, electrification and dieselisation merely served to push 'Schools' and

Moguls farther west, and in Scotland, displaced 'A4s' exploited their potential when they took over the Glasgow-Aberdeen run. The author is not aware of any division or district on BR which ever became totally dependent on BR Standard steam locomotives for its operations.

Many observers have commented that towards the end of steam, locomotives became run-down as a result of a decline in maintenance and cleaning standards. While this clearly did happen in some depots, and indeed there is a sound psychological reason why this might have been so, it was in fact by no means universally the case. Certainly some Western locomotives reached a very sad visual state: cabside numberplates, nameplates and even the brass safety valve covers, were sometimes seen to be missing, signs that they were no longer loved. It had never been uncommon to see dirty engines on the London Midland and Eastern Regions, but some of the steam leaks that escaped attention in the last couple of years in some places did border on the excessive. The pictures which accompany this chapter are a fair cross-section of what could be seen in the last four years of steam operation on BR. They include some reminders that many depots kept their engines clean and mechanically 'tight' right up to the end.

The last main line to use steam locomotives on top link passenger turns was that from Waterloo to Bournemouth and Weymouth. 1967 was the year, and enthusiast attention to the route was high, reaching a crescendo in the few weeks before the last day on 9 July. For several years before, the SR had set up Guildford depot as a centre for specialist maintenance work such as valves and pistons examinations. To an extent as a result of this work, the mechanical condition of Southern engines actually improved. Thus there were many excellent performances possible from the last rebuilt 'Merchant Navy' and 'West Country' locomotives in the hands of drivers having a last fling: 100mph running was reported by the travelling fans on several occasions. Even the few remaining unrebuilt Bulleid Pacifics did some good running, backed by the ever-willing BR Standard Class 5s. The only sad sign of the impending end of the work of the steam engine cleaner was the layer of grime which spread across these great steam machines in the last months of their extremely active lives. Even that had its advantage to a few. It was more effective than shiny paint as a base for the inevitable chalked epitaphs which adorned the last steam locomotives on their last runs!

A feature of these years was the heightening popularity of special trains for enthusiasts. In the early 1960s the object of many tours had been visits to closing branch lines or secondary routes. Now the emphasis was on a last chance to ride behind a favourite steam locomotive, or to parade an engine in areas which it had never visited before. Thus an 'A3' went to Bournemouth, an 'A4' visited Weymouth, and a 'Merchant Navy' broke records on the climb to Ais Gill summit. One can recall more than one last chance to ride behind a 'Castle'! The official 'last steam' runs to Bournemouth were held at least a week before the actual last day!

When the Southern's last steam engines had made their final, funereal trips to Weymouth and Salisbury depots in the dark of that Sunday night in July 1967, there remained only one area worked by steam on BR. The lines radiating from Preston and Manchester, fed by the depots at Carnforth, Lostock Hall and Buxton, became the pilgrim centre for steam fans. Thus the last steam enthusiasts concentrated their massed cameras on stone trains being hauled up the Pennines by clanking '8Fs' in the snow, or they waited for a less-than-certain Class 5 to appear on a local passenger train at Preston. The last steam locomotives on BR were mostly LMS Class 5s and '8Fs', with a few Standard Class 4s and 5s supporting them. Crewe works surprisingly outshopped No 70013 *Oliver Cromwell*

after a late overhaul, but did not line out its green paintwork.

Then came the last specials, the end of steam on British Rail. A high fare was charged, but many paid to ride behind No 70013, and behind a pair of 'Black 5s', Nos 44871 and 44781, and lastly behind No 45110. Then everyone believed it was all over.

During these years the merchants whose yards scrapped old railway equipment had been having a boom time. The last years saw thousands of engines broken up for scrap. Visitors to these places saw their favourites standing gaunt, rusty, and with signs that the cutter's torch had begun its work. The value of scrap copper and steel enhanced the urgency of the work. In a remarkably short time most of the relics had disappeared, cut into unrecognisable chunks of twisted metal and dropped into some blast furnace somewhere to be recycled, most likely as not to become cars or washing machines — except at one location in Wales.

Maybe it was the slower pace of life in that principality, or maybe Dai Woodham had his eye on an investment: whatever the reason, over 200 steam locomotives stood on the site of Woodham's scrapyard on Barry Island and most escaped the torch. A few engines had been purchased directly from British Rail by steam railways and individuals, but the story of how and why one man saved so many more for posterity will no doubt be told in good time.

*Above:*
**As the twilight of steam's reign on British Railways approaches, red Pacific No 46256 *Sir William A. Stanier, FRS* stands under the wires at Glasgow Central in April 1964.** *D. Cameron/Colour-Rail SC195*

*Top right:*
**This pre-Grouping 0-6-0 had been repainted as late as 1966! Class J27 No 65842 is seen at Woodburn with the Thursdays only goods from Morpeth in September of that year.** *J. M. Boyes/Colour-Rail BRE222*

*Bottom right:*
**Two outwardly ill-kempt BR Class 4 4-6-0s Nos 75053 and 75063, make a fine picture as they breast Talerddig summit in December 1965 with the up 'Cambrian Coast Express'.** *T. B. Owen/Colour-Rail BRW517*

Steam reigned supreme in the North-west while other areas
succumbed to diesel or electric traction. On Ais Gill Viaduct,
2-10-0 No 92017 heads an up freight in September 1965.
*A. E. R. Cope/Colour-Rail BRM536*

Class 5 4-6-0 No 44795 surmounts the summit of the Settle & Carlisle line at Ais Gill with a freight in May 1966.
*A. E. R. Cope/Colour-Rail BRM 193*

*Above:*

**A feature of the last months of steam working was the appearance of engines well away from their normal spheres of operation, as available motive power was used to the best advantage. This strange face at Doncaster is 'Black 5' No 45208 which had arrived in February 1967 with the 20.20 from Bradford.** *G. Warnes/Colour-Rail BRE517*

*Below:*

**St Pancras station is the background to this classic shot of 'Jubilee' 4-6-0 No 45721 *Impregnable* awaiting departure with an enthusiasts' special.** *R. Hill/Colour-Rail BRM161*

*Above:*

**December 1964 produced sufficient snow for this delightful scene on the Cambrian main line. Ex-GW 4-6-0 No 7827 *Lydham Manor* climbs towards Talerddig with the up 'Cambrian Coast Express'.** *T. B. Owen/Colour-Rail BRW450*

*Left:*

**Extreme cold weather was not ideal for efficient steam locomotive operation! In this photograph taken in the winter of 1963, BR Class 5 4-6-0 No 73093 appears to be in control as it starts an up local on the former LSWR main line at Farnborough.** *T. B. Owen/Colour-Rail BRS431*

*Left:*

**Preston was one of the last major BR stations to be served by steam. In its LNW trainshed. Class 5-4-6-0 No 44892 pauses with a parcels train in February 1966.**
*B. Magilton/Colour-Rail BRM601*

The Isle of Wight system retained steam operation with ex-LSWR Class O2 0-4-4Ts right up to electrification in 1966. Not long before the end of steam there, No W22 *Brading* climbs past Smallbrook Junction near Ryde with a train for the Shanklin line. *J. G. Dewing/Colour-Rail BRS478*

In the summer of 1964 another load of holidaymakers going south in the 'Pines Express' to Bournemouth are hauled at speed past Shawford by clean rebuilt 'West Country' 4-6-2 No 34017 Ilfracombe. *B. J. Swain/Colour-Rail BRS425*

*Above:*

**Many BR tank engines were sold to other concerns when no longer required. Among these was GW pannier tank No 7760 which became No L90 of London Transport, seen here shunting at Watford tip in January 1968.**
*P. Zabek/Colour-Rail LT19*

*Left:*

**No 80103 was the first BR Class 4 2-6-4T to be withdrawn for scrap. It stands here forlorn, at the head of a row of ex-Great Eastern 'J15' 0-6-0s at Stratford in 1962.**
*Colin Boocock*

*Left:*

**All-out effort! LMS Class 8F 2-8-0 No 48532 makes an explosively evocative sight (not to say sound) as it heads a Tunstead empty stone train near Buxworth in February 1968.** *W. Chapman/Colour-Rail BRM541*

# APPENDICES
## 1 British Railways Steam Classes 1948 and 1961

**Ex-LNER types**

| Class | Wheel Arrangement | Origin | Number in Class 1948 | 1961 | Class | Wheel Arrangement | Origin | Number in Class 1948 | 1961 |
|-------|-------------------|--------|----------------------|------|-------|-------------------|--------|----------------------|------|
| A1 | 4-6-2 | LNER/BR | 4 | 50 | F6 | 2-4-2T | GER | 22 | — |
| A2 | 4-6-2 | LNER | 40 | 30 | F7 | 2-4-2T | GER | 2 | — |
| A3 | 4-6-2 | LNER | 77 | 76 | G5 | 0-4-4T | NER | 109 | — |
| A4 | 4-6-2 | LNER | 34 | 34 | J1 | 0-6-0 | GNR | 11 | — |
| A5 | 4-6-2T | GCR | 43 | — | J2 | 0-6-0 | GNR | 9 | — |
| A6 | 4-6-2T | NER | 9 | — | J3 | 0-6-0 | GNR | 30 | — |
| A7 | 4-6-2T | NER | 20 | — | J4 | 0-6-0 | GNR | 4 | — |
| A8 | 4-6-2T | NER | 45 | — | J5 | 0-6-0 | GNR | 20 | — |
| A10 | 4-6-2 | GNR | 1 | — | J6 | 0-6-0 | GNR | 110 | 10 |
| B1 | 4-6-0 | LNER | 340 | 409 | J10 | 0-6-0 | MSLR | 77 | 2 |
| B2 | 4-6-0 | LNER | 9 | — | J11 | 0-6-0 | GCR | 174 | 33 |
| B3 | 4-6-0 | GCR | 1 | — | J15 | 0-6-0 | GER | 116 | 14 |
| B4 | 4-6-0 | GCR | 4 | — | J17 | 0-6-0 | GER | 89 | 15 |
| B5 | 4-6-0 | GCR | 4 | — | J19 | 0-6-0 | GER | 35 | 8 |
| B7 | 4-6-0 | GCR | 25 | — | J20 | 0-6-0 | GER | 25 | 9 |
| B8 | 4-6-0 | GCR | 2 | — | J21 | 0-6-0 | NER | 77 | 2 |
| B9 | 4-6-0 | GCR | 3 | — | J24 | 0-6-0 | NER | 31 | — |
| B12 | 4-6-0 | GER | 71 | 1 | J25 | 0-6-0 | NER | 74 | 9 |
| B13 | 4-6-0 | NER | 1 | — | J26 | 0-6-0 | NER | 50 | 17 |
| B16 | 4-6-0 | NER | 69 | 44 | J27 | 0-6-0 | NER | 115 | 92 |
| B17 'Sandringham' | 4-6-0 | LNER | 61 | — | J35 | 0-6-0 | NBR | 70 | 5 |
| C1 | 4-4-2 | GNR | 10 | — | J36 | 0-6-0 | NBR | 118 | 69 |
| C4 | 4-4-2 | GCR | 15 | — | J37 | 0-6-0 | NBR | 104 | 98 |
| C7 | 4-4-2 | NER | 2 | — | J38 | 0-6-0 | LNER | 35 | 35 |
| C12 | 4-4-2T | GNR | 44 | — | J39 | 0-6-0 | LNER | 289 | 141 |
| C13 | 4-4-2T | GCR | 40 | — | J50 | 0-6-0T | GNR | 102 | 40 |
| C14 | 4-4-2T | GCR | 12 | — | J52 | 0-6-0ST | GNR | 133 | — |
| C15 | 4-4-2T | NBR | 30 | — | J55 | 0-6-0ST | GNR | 2 | — |
| C16 | 4-4-2T | NBR | 21 | — | J62 | 0-6-0ST | GCR | 3 | — |
| D1 | 4-4-0 | GNR | 7 | — | J63 | 0-6-0T | GCR | 7 | — |
| D2 | 4-4-0 | GNR | 26 | — | J65 | 0-6-0T | GER | 3 | — |
| D3 | 4-4-0 | GNR | 15 | — | J66 | 0-6-0T | GER | 19 | 1 |
| D9 | 4-4-0 | GCR | 26 | — | J67 | 0-6-0T | GER | 45 | — |
| D10 'Director' | 4-4-0 | GCR | 10 | — | J68 | 0-6-0T | GER | 29 | 3 |
| D11 'Large Director' | 4-4-0 | GCR | 34 | 5 | J69 | 0-6-0T | GER | 89 | 20 |
| D15 'Claud Hamilton' | 4-4-0 | GER | 12 | — | J70 | 0-6-0Tram | GER | 11 | — |
| D16 'Super Claud' | 4-4-0 | GER | 102 | — | J71 | 0-6-0T | NER | 81 | — |
| D20 | 4-4-0 | NER | 49 | — | J72 | 0-6-0T | NER | 81 | 59 |
| D29 'Scott' | 4-4-0 | NBR | 10 | — | J73 | 0-6-0T | NER | 10 | — |
| D30 'Scott' | 4-4-0 | NBR | 25 | — | J75 | 0-6-0T | HBR | 1 | — |
| D31 | 4-4-0 | NBR | 4 | — | J77 | 0-6-0T | NER | 45 | — |
| D32 | 4-4-0 | NBR | 5 | — | J83 | 0-6-0T | NBR | 39 | 11 |
| D33 | 4-4-0 | NBR | 9 | — | J88 | 0-6-0T | NBR | 35 | 8 |
| D34 'Glen' | 4-4-0 | NBR | 30 | 3 | J92 | 0-6-0CT | GER | 3 | — |
| D40 | 4-4-0 | GNSR | 18 | 1 | J93 | 0-6-0T | MGNJR | 1 | — |
| D41 | 4-4-0 | GNSR | 21 | — | J94 | 0-6-0ST | WD | 75 | 66 |
| D49 'Shire'/'Hunt' | 4-4-0 | LNER | 76 | — | K1 | 2-6-0 | LNER/BR | 1 | 70 |
| E4 | 2-4-0 | GER | 18 | — | K2 | 2-6-0 | GNR | 75 | 3 |
| F1 | 2-4-2T | MSLR | 2 | — | K3 | 2-6-0 | LNER | 192 | 142 |
| F2 | 2-4-2T | GCR | 8 | — | K4 | 2-6-0 | LNER | 5 | 5 |
| F3 | 2-4-2T | GER | 8 | — | K5 | 2-6-0 | LNER | 1 | — |
| F4 | 2-4-2T | GER | 26 | — | L1 | 2-6-4T | LNER | 30 | 79 |
| F5 | 2-4-2T | GER | 30 | — | L2 | 2-6-4T | Met | 2 | — |
|   |   |   |   |   | L3 | 2-6-4T | GCR | 19 | — |
|   |   |   |   |   | M2 | 0-6-4T | Met | 2 | — |
|   |   |   |   |   | N1 | 0-6-2T | GNR | 55 | — |

| Class | Wheel Arrangement | Origin | 1948 | 1961 |
|---|---|---|---|---|
| N2 | 0-6-2T | GNR | 107 | 20 |
| N4 | 0-6-2T | MSLR | 22 | — |
| N5 | 0-6-2T | MSLR | 121 | — |
| N7 | 0-6-2T | GER | 134 | 25 |
| N8 | 0-6-2T | NER | 30 | — |
| N9 | 0-6-2T | NER | 16 | — |
| N10 | 0-6-2T | NER | 20 | 3 |
| N13 | 0-6-2T | HBR | 9 | — |
| N14 | 0-6-2T | NBR | 3 | — |
| N15 | 0-6-2T | NBR | 99 | 24 |
| O1 | 2-8-0 | GCR/LNER | 52 | 58 |
| O2 | 2-8-0 | GNR | 66 | 56 |
| O3 | 2-8-0 | GNR | 15 | — |
| O4 | 2-8-0 | GCR | 277 | 202 |
| O7* | 2-8-0 | WD | 200 | — |
| Q1 | 0-8-0T | GCR | 13 | — |
| Q4 | 0-8-0 | GCR | 34 | — |
| Q5 | 0-8-0 | NER | 66 | — |
| Q6 | 0-8-0 | NER | 120 | 119 |
| Q7 | 0-8-0 | NER | 15 | 15 |
| S1 | 0-8-4T | GCR | 6 | — |
| T1 | 4-8-0T | NER | 13 | — |
| U1 | 2-8-0+0-8-2T | LNER | 1 | — |
| V1 | 2-6-2T | LNER | 78 | 17 |
| V2 | 2-6-2 | LNER | 184 | 184 |
| V3 | 2-6-2T | LNER | 14 | 67 |
| V4 | 2-6-2 | LNER | 2 | — |
| W1 | 4-6-4 | LNER | 1 | — |
| Y1 | 0-4-0T | Sentinel | 23 | 1 |
| Y3 | 0-4-0T | Sentinel | 31 | 3 |
| Y4 | 0-4-0T | GER | 5 | 1 |
| Y6 | 0-4-0Tram | GER | 2 | — |
| Y7 | 0-4-0T | NER | 2 | — |
| Y8 | 0-4-0T | NER | 2 | — |
| Y9 | 0-4-0ST | NBR | 33 | 6 |
| Y10 | 0-4-0T | Sentinel | 1 | — |
| Z4 | 0-4-2T | GNSR | 2 | — |
| Z5 | 0-4-2T | GNSR | 2 | — |

**Number of classes:** 146 55

**Number of locomotives:** 6,424 2,520

*See also WD 2-8-0, ex-War Department classes.

**Key:**

| | |
|---|---|
| BR | British Railways |
| GCR | Great Central Railway |
| GER | Great Eastern Railway |
| GNR | Great Northern Railway |
| GNSR | Great North of Scotland Railway |
| HBR | Hull & Barnsley Railway |
| LNER | London & North Eastern Railway |
| Met | Metropolitan Railway |
| MGNJR | Midland & Great Northern Joint Railway |
| MSLR | Manchester, Sheffield & Lincoln Railway |
| NBR | North British Railway |
| NER | North Eastern Railway |
| WD | War Department |

**Ex-LMS types**

| Class | Wheel Arrangement | Origin | 1948 | 1961 |
|---|---|---|---|---|
| 7P/8P 'Princess Royal' | 4-6-2 | LMS | 13 | 12 |
| 7P/8P 'Coronation' | 4-6-2 | LMS | 38 | 38 |
| 6P/7P 'Rebuilt Scot' | 4-6-0 | LMS | 47 | 71 |
| 6P/7P 'Royal Scot' | 4-6-0 | LMS | 24 | — |
| 6P/7P 'Rebuilt Jubilee' | 4-6-0 | LMS | 2 | 2 |
| 6P/7P 'Rebuilt Patriot' | 4-6-0 | LMS | 10 | 17 |

| Class | Wheel Arrangement | Origin | 1948 | 1961 |
|---|---|---|---|---|
| 5XP/6P 'Jubilee' | 4-6-0 | LMS | 189 | 185 |
| 5XP/6P 'Patriot' | 4-6-0 | LMS | 42 | 27 |
| 5XP 'Claughton' | 4-6-0 | LNWR | 1 | — |
| 5 | 4-6-0 | LMS | 802 | 842 |
| 5P | 4-6-0 | LYR | 5 | — |
| 4P 'Prince of Wales' | 4-6-0 | LNWR | 3 | — |
| 4F Whale '19in Goods' | 4-6-0 | LNWR | 3 | — |
| 4P | 4-6-0 | CR | 5 | — |
| 4P | 4-6-0 | LMS/CR | 14 | — |
| 4P 'Clan' | 4-6-0 | HR | 1 | — |
| 4F 'Clan Goods' | 4-6-0 | HR | 6 | — |
| 4P 'Compound' | 4-4-0 | MR | 40 | 1 |
| 4P 'Compound' | 4-4-0 | LMS | 195 | — |
| 3P 'Precursor' | 4-4-0 | LNWR | 1 | — |
| 3P | 4-4-0 | MR | 18 | — |
| 3P Class 928 | 4-4-0 | CR | 16 | 4 |
| 3P Class 72 | 4-4-0 | CR | 32 | 13 |
| 3P 'Dunalastair IV' rebuilt | 4-4-0 | CR | 2 | — |
| 3P 'Dunalastair IV' | 4-4-0 | CR | 20 | — |
| 2P | 4-4-0 | MR | 165 | 3 |
| 2P | 4-4-0 | LMS | 136 | 49 |
| 2P | 4-4-0 | CR | 1 | — |
| 2P 'Loch' | 4-4-0 | HR | 1 | — |
| 2P 'Ben' | 4-4-0 | HR | 8 | — |
| — Beyer Garratt | 2-6-0+0-6-2T | LMS | 33 | — |
| — | 0-10-0 | MR | 1 | — |
| 8F | 2-8-0 | LMS | 624 | 665 |
| 7F | 2-8-0 | SDJR | 11 | 7 |
| 5F Hughes | 2-6-0 | LMS | 245 | 242 |
| 5F Stanier | 2-6-0 | LMS | 40 | 40 |
| 4F Ivatt | 2-6-0 | LMS | 40 | 162 |
| 2F Ivatt | 2-6-0 | LMS | 35 | 128 |
| 1P 6ft 9in | 2-4-0 | MR | 1 | — |
| 1P 6ft 3in | 2-4-0 | MR | 1 | — |
| 7F | 0-8-0 | LMS | 175 | 4 |
| 7F G2a | 0-8-0 | LNWR | 320 | 90 |
| 7F G2 | 0-8-0 | LNWR | 60 | 41 |
| 6F G1 | 0-8-0 | LNWR | 98 | — |
| 7F | 0-8-0 | LYR | 14 | — |
| 6F | 0-8-0 | LYR | 11 | — |
| 4F | 0-6-0 | MR | 192 | 100 |
| 4F | 0-6-0 | LMS | 580 | 482 |
| 3F Aspinall | 0-6-0 | LYR | 235 | 1 |
| 3F Hughes | 0-6-0 | LYR | 35 | 17 |
| 3F | 0-6-0 | MR | 11 | 1 |
| 3F | 0-6-0 | SDJR | 9 | 1 |
| 3F Johnson | 0-6-0 | MR | 317 | 61 |
| 3F Deeley | 0-6-0 | MR | 54 | 7 |
| 3F | 0-6-0 | FR | 6 | — |
| 3F Class 812/652 | 0-6-0 | CR | 89 | 62 |
| 3F Class 294 | 0-6-0 | CR | 23 | 22 |
| 3F Class 670 | 0-6-0 | CR | 6 | 6 |
| 3F | 0-6-0 | HR | 7 | — |
| 2F | 0-6-0 | LNWR | 58 | — |
| 2F | 0-6-0 | LNWR | 35 | — |
| 2F | 0-6-0 | LYR | 23 | — |
| 2F Johnson | 0-6-0 | MR | 95 | 18 |
| 2F Johnson | 0-6-0 | MR | 93 | 3 |
| 2F Kirtley | 0-6-0 | MR | 4 | — |
| 2F | 0-6-0 | CR | 222 | 106 |
| 4P | 4-6-2T | CR | 9 | — |
| 3P | 4-4-2T | LTSR | 51 | — |
| 2P | 4-4-2T | LTSR | 17 | — |
| 4P Fairburn | 2-6-4T | LMS | 180 | 277 |
| 4P Stanier | 2-6-4T | LMS | 206 | 202 |
| 4P Stanier 3-cyl | 2-6-4T | LMS | 37 | 33 |
| 4P Fowler | 2-6-4T | LMS | 125 | 104 |
| 3P Stanier | 2-6-2T | LMS | 139 | 120 |
| 3P Fowler | 2-6-2T | LMS | 70 | 3 |

| Class | Wheel Arrangement | Origin | 1948 | 1961 |
|---|---|---|---|---|
| 2P Ivatt | 2-6-2T | LMS | 30 | 130 |
| 3P | 2-4-2T | LYR | 8 | — |
| 2P | 2-4-2T | LYR | 105 | 1 |
| 1P | 2-4-2T | LNWR | 30 | — |
| 1P | 2-4-0T | LNWR | 1 | — |
| 7F | 0-8-4T | LNWR | 10 | — |
| 6F | 0-8-2T | LNWR | 8 | — |
| 3F | 0-6-2T | LTSR | 14 | 1 |
| 2P | 0-6-2T | LNWR | 9 | — |
| 2F | 0-6-2T | LNWR | 50 | — |
| 3F | 0-6-0T | LMS | 412 | 325 |
| 3F | 0-6-0T | MR | 60 | 22 |
| 3F | 0-6-0T | CR | 147 | 14 |
| 2F | 0-6-0T | LMS | 10 | 7 |
| 2F | 0-6-0T | NLR | 14 | — |
| 2F | 0-6-0T | CR | 23 | 2 |
| 1F | 0-6-0T | LYR | 5 | 1 |
| 1F | 0-6-0T | MR | 87 | 11 |
| 2F | 0-6-0ST | LNWR | 1 | — |
| 2F | 0-6-0ST | LYR | 95 | 13 |
| 2P | 0-4-4T | LMS | 10 | 1 |
| 2P | 0-4-4T | LMS/CR | 10 | 1 |
| 2P Class 431 | 0-4-4T | CR | 4 | 2 |
| 2P Class 439 | 0-4-4T | CR | 74 | 29 |
| 2P Class 19 | 0-4-4T | CR | 24 | 1 |
| 1P | 0-4-4T | MR | 8 | — |
| 1P | 0-4-4T | MR | 51 | — |
| 0P | 0-4-4T | HR | 2 | — |
| 1F | 0-4-2ST | LNWR | 2 | — |
| — | 0-4-2CT | NLR | 1 | — |
| 0F | 0-4-0T | MR | 10 | 5 |
| — Sentinel | 0-4-0T | LMS | 7 | — |
| — Railmotor | 0-4-0T | LNWR | 1 | — |
| 0F | 0-4-0ST | LMS | 5 | 10 |
| 0F | 0-4-0ST | LYR | 23 | 12 |
| 0F | 0-4-0ST | MR | 3 | — |
| 0F | 0-4-0ST | CR | 14 | 3 |
| — | 4-6-0 | HR | — | 1 |
| — | 4-2-2 | CR | — | 1 |

**Number of classes:** 112   64

**Number of locomotives:** 7,805   4,862

**Key:**

| | |
|---|---|
| CR | Caledonian Railway |
| FR | Furness Railway |
| HR | Highland Railway |
| LMS | London, Midland & Scottish Railway |
| LNWR | London & North Western Railway |
| LTSR | London, Tilbury & Southend Railway |
| LYR | Lancashire & Yorkshire Railway |
| MR | Midland Railway |
| SDJR | Somerset & Dorset Joint Railway |

**Ex-SR Types:**

| Class | Wheel Arrangement | Origin | 1948 | 1961 |
|---|---|---|---|---|
| A1 'Terrier' | 0-6-0T | LBSCR | 1 | 1 |
| A1X 'Terrier' | 0-6-0T | LBSCR | 14 | 10 |
| A12 | 0-4-2 | LSWR | 2 | — |
| B1 | 4-4-0 | SECR | 11 | — |
| B4 | 0-4-0T | LSWR | 22 | 3 |
| B4 | 4-4-0 | LBSCR | 6 | — |
| B4X | 4-4-0 | LBSCR | 12 | — |
| C | 0-6-0 | SECR | 106 | 38 |
| C2 | 0-6-0 | LBSCR | 2 | — |
| C2X | 0-6-0 | LBSCR | 45 | 20 |
| C3 | 0-6-0 | LBSCR | 8 | — |
| C14 | 0-4-0T | LSWR | 3 | — |
| D | 4-4-0 | SECR | 28 | — |
| D1 | 4-4-0 | SECR | 20 | 5 |
| D1 | 0-4-2T | LBSCR | 13 | — |
| D3 | 0-4-4T | LBSCR | 26 | — |
| D15 | 4-4-0 | LSWR | 10 | — |

| Class | Wheel Arrangement | Origin | 1948 | 1961 |
|---|---|---|---|---|
| E | 4-4-0 | SECR | 15 | — |
| E1 | 4-4-0 | SECR | 11 | 1 |
| E1 | 0-6-0T | LBSCR | 26 | — |
| E1/R | 0-6-2T | LBSCR | 10 | — |
| E2 | 0-6-2T | LBSCR | 10 | 8 |
| E3 | 0-6-2T | LBSCR | 16 | — |
| E4 | 0-6-2T | LBSCR | 70 | 19 |
| E4X | 0-6-2T | LBSCR | 4 | — |
| E5 | 0-6-2T | LBSCR | 24 | — |
| E5X | 0-6-2T | LBSCR | 4 | — |
| E6 | 0-6-2T | LBSCR | 10 | 5 |
| E6X | 0-6-2T | LBSCR | 2 | — |
| F1 | 4-4-0 | SECR | 4 | — |
| G6 | 0-6-0T | LSWR | 32 | 2 |
| G16 | 4-8-0T | LSWR | 4 | 2 |
| H | 0-4-4T | SECR | 63 | 21 |
| H1 | 4-4-2 | LBSCR | 3 | — |
| H2 | 4-4-2 | LBSCR | 6 | — |
| H15 | 4-6-0 | LSWR/SR | 26 | 5 |
| H16 | 4-6-2T | LSWR | 5 | 5 |
| I1X | 4-4-2T | LBSCR | 9 | — |
| I3 | 4-4-2T | LBSCR | 26 | — |
| J | 0-6-4T | SECR | 5 | — |
| J1 | 4-6-2T | LBSCR | 1 | — |
| J2 | 4-6-2T | LBSCR | 1 | — |
| K | 2-6-0 | LBSCR | 17 | 17 |
| K10 | 4-4-0 | LSWR | 23 | — |
| KESR | 0-8-0T | KESR | 1 | — |
| L | 4-4-0 | SECR | 22 | 2 |
| L1 | 4-4-0 | SR | 15 | 8 |
| L11 | 4-4-0 | LSWR | 40 | — |
| L12 | 4-4-0 | LSWR | 20 | — |
| LN 'Lord Nelson' | 4-6-0 | SR | 16 | 14 |
| M7 | 0-4-4T | LSWR | 103 | 57 |
| 'Merchant Navy' | 4-6-2 | SR | 30 | — |
| 'Merchant Navy' rebuilt | 4-6-2 | SR/BR | — | 30 |
| N | 2-6-0 | SECR | 80 | 80 |
| N1 | 2-6-0 | SECR | 6 | 6 |
| N15 'King Arthur' | 4-6-0 | LSWR/SR | 74 | 18 |
| N15X 'Remembrance' | 4-6-0 | LBSCR/SR | 7 | — |
| O1 | 0-6-0 | SECR | 46 | — |
| O2 | 0-4-4T | LSWR | 48 | 25 |
| P | 0-6-0T | SECR | 8 | 8 |
| Q | 0-6-0 | SR | 20 | 20 |
| Q1 | 0-6-0 | SR | 40 | 40 |
| R | 0-4-4T | SECR | 15 | — |
| R1 | 0-4-4T | SECR | 13 | — |
| R1 | 0-6-0T | SECR | 9 | — |
| S | 0-6-0ST | SECR | 1 | — |
| S11 | 4-4-0 | LSWR | 10 | — |
| S15 | 4-6-0 | LSWR/SR | 45 | 45 |
| T | 0-6-0T | SECR | 3 | — |
| T1 | 0-4-4T | LSWR | 9 | — |
| T9 | 4-4-0 | LSWR | 66 | 2 |
| T14 | 4-6-0 | LSWR | 9 | — |
| U | 2-6-0 | SECR | 50 | 50 |
| U1 | 2-6-0 | SR | 21 | 21 |
| V 'Schools' | 4-4-0 | SR | 40 | 34 |
| W | 2-6-4T | SR | 15 | 15 |
| 'West Country'/ 'Battle of Britain' | 4-6-2 | SR | 90 | 50 |
| 'West Country'/ 'Battle of Britain' rebuilt | 4-6-2 | SR/BR | — | 60 |
| Z | 0-8-0T | SR | 8 | 8 |
| 700 | 0-6-0 | LSWR | 30 | 18 |
| 756 | 0-6-0T | PDSWJR | 1 | — |
| 757 | 0-6-2T | PDSWJR | 2 | — |
| 1302 | 0-4-0CT | SECR | 1 | — |
| 0298 | 2-4-0WT | LSWR | 3 | 3 |
| 0395 | 0-6-0 | LSWR | 18 | — |
| 0458 | 0-4-0ST | LSWR | 1 | — |
| 0415 | 4-4-2T | LSWR | 3 | — |

| Class | Wheel Arrangement | Origin | Number in Class 1948 | 1961 |
|---|---|---|---|---|
| USA | 0-6-0T | USATC | 14 | 14 |
| 30948 | 0-6-0T | EKR | 1 | — |
| 'Leader' | 0-6-6-0T | SR/BR | † | — |
| **Number of classes:** | | | 87 | 39 |
| **Number of locomotives:** | | | 1,810 | 782 |

†Five locomotives built (four not commissioned) 1949; all scrapped 1950-51.

**Key:**

| | |
|---|---|
| BR | British Railways |
| EKR | East Kent Railway |
| KESR | Kent & East Sussex Railway |
| LBSCR | London, Brighton & South Coast Railway |
| LSWR | London & South Western Railway |
| PDSWJR | Plymouth, Devonport & South Western Junction Railway |
| SECR | South Eastern & Chatham Railway (incorporating South Eastern Railway and London, Chatham & Dover Railway) |
| SR | Southern Railway |
| USATC | United States Army Transportation Corps |

**Ex-GWR Types:**

| Class | Wheel Arrangement | Origin | Number in Class 1948 | 1961 |
|---|---|---|---|---|
| 517 | 0-4-2T | GWR | 3 | — |
| 10XX | 4-6-0 | GWR | 30 | 30 |
| 1101 | 0-4-0T | GWR | 6 | — |
| 1361 | 0-6-0ST | GWR | 5 | 2 |
| 1366 | 0-6-0PT | GWR | 6 | 3 |
| 14XX | 0-4-2T | GWR | 95 | 28 |
| 15XX | 0-6-0PT | GWR/BR | — | 7 |
| 1501 | 0-6-0PT | GWR | 9 | — |
| 16XX | 0-6-0PT | GWR/BR | — | 51 |
| 1701 | 0-6-0PT | GWR | 27 | — |
| 1813 | 0-6-0PT | GWR | 1 | — |
| 1901 | 0-6-0PT | GWR | 44 | — |
| 2021 | 0-6-0PT | GWR | 110 | — |
| 2251 | 0-6-0 | GWR | 120 | 80 |
| 2301 | 0-6-0 | GWR | 53 | — |
| 26XX 'Aberdare' | 2-6-0 | GWR | 4 | — |
| 27XX | 0-6-0PT | GWR | 40 | — |
| 28XX | 2-8-0 | GWR | 167 | 117 |
| 29XX 'Saint' | 4-6-0 | GWR | 41 | — |
| 31XX | 2-6-2T | GWR | 5 | — |
| 3150 | 2-6-2T | GWR | 30 | — |
| 3252 'Duke' | 4-4-0 | GWR | 11 | — |
| 33XX 'Bulldog' | 4-4-0 | GWR | 34 | — |
| 35XX | 2-4-0T | GWR | 7 | — |
| 40XX 'Star' | 4-6-0 | GWR | 46 | — |
| 4073 'Castle' | 4-6-0 | GWR | 151 | 155 |
| 42XX | 2-8-0T | GWR | 151 | 130 |
| 43XX | 2-6-0 | GWR | 235 | 121 |
| 44XX | 2-6-2T | GWR | 11 | — |
| 45XX | 2-6-2T | GWR | 175 | 53 |
| 47XX | 2-8-0 | GWR | 9 | 9 |
| 49XX 'Hall' | 4-6-0 | GWR | 258 | 251 |
| 51XX | 2-6-2T | GWR | 148 | 96 |
| 54XX | 0-6-0PT | GWR | 25 | 5 |
| 56XX | 0-6-2T | GWR | 200 | 200 |
| 57XX | 0-6-0PT | GWR | 831 | 608 |
| 60XX 'King' | 4-6-0 | GWR | 30 | 30 |
| 61XX | 2-6-2T | GWR | 70 | 65 |
| 64XX | 0-6-0PT | GWR | 40 | 22 |
| 68XX 'Grange' | 4-6-0 | GWR | 80 | 77 |
| 6959 'Modified Hall' | 4-6-0 | GWR | 32 | 71 |
| 72XX | 2-8-2T | GWR | 54 | 54 |
| 74XX | 0-6-0PT | GWR | 35 | 37 |
| 78XX 'Manor' | 4-6-0 | GWR | 20 | 30 |
| 81XX | 2-6-2T | GWR | 10 | 7 |

| Class | Wheel Arrangement | Origin | Number in Class 1948 | 1961 |
|---|---|---|---|---|
| 90XX 'Dukedog' | 4-4-0 | GWR | 27 | — |
| 94XX | 0-6-0PT | GWR | 10 | 154 |
| 30XX 'ROD'* | 2-8-0 | ROD | 32 | — |
| — | 0-4-0ST | YTW | 1 | — |
| — | 0-4-2ST | Corris | 1 | — |
| — | 0-4-2ST | Corris | 1 | — |
| — | 0-6-0T | WCPR | 1 | — |
| † | 2-6-2T | VoR | 3 | 3 |
| — | 0-6-2T | BMR | 13 | — |
| — | 0-6-0T | CMDPR | 2 | — |
| — | 0-6-2T | RR | 49 | — |
| — | 0-6-0T | RR | 7 | — |
| — | 0-6-2T | Cardiff | 1 | — |
| — | 0-6-0T | Cardiff | 4 | — |
| — | 0-4-0ST | Cardiff | 1 | 1 |
| — | 0-6-2T | PTR | 1 | — |
| — | 0-6-2T | TVR | 95 | — |
| — | 0-6-0T | TVR | 3 | — |
| — | 0-6-2T | Barry | 16 | — |
| — | 0-6-0T | Barry | 1 | — |
| — | 0-6-0ST | LMMR | 1 | — |
| — | 0-6-0T | ADR | 3 | — |
| — | 2-6-2T | ADR | 2 | — |
| — | 0-4-0ST | PM | 4 | 1 |
| — | 0-6-0T | WLR | 2 | — |
| — | 0-6-0 | Cambrian | 11 | — |
| — | 0-4-0ST | SHT | 6 | — |
| — | 0-6-0ST | SHT | 3 | — |
| — | 2-4-0 | MSWJR | 3 | — |
| — | 0-6-0T | WCR | 1 | — |
| — | 0-6-0T | BPGVR | 6 | — |
| — | 0-6-0T | BPGVR | 7 | — |
| **Number of classes:** | | | 73 | 32 |
| **Number of locomotives:** | | | 3,777 | 2,499 |

*See also ex-LNER Class O4.
†See also ex-LBSCR Class A1X.

**Key:**

| | |
|---|---|
| ADR | Alexandra Dock Railway |
| Barry | Barry Railway |
| BMR | Brecon & Merthyr Railway |
| BPGVR | Burry Port & Gwendraeth Valley Railway |
| BR | British Railways |
| Cambrian | Cambrian Railways |
| Cardiff | Cardiff Railway |
| CMDPR | Cleobury Mortimer & Ditton Priors Railway |
| Corris | Corris Railway |
| LMMR | Llanelli & Mynydd Mawr Railway |
| MSWJR | Midland & South Western Junction Railway |
| PM | Powesland & Mason |
| PTR | Port Talbot Railway |
| ROD | Royal Ordnance Department |
| RR | Rhymney Railway |
| SHT | Swansea Harbour Trust |
| TVR | Taff Vale Railway |
| VoR | Vale of Rheidol Railway |
| WLR | Welshpool & Llanfair Railway |
| WCPR | Weston, Cleveland & Portishead Railway |
| WCR | Whitland & Cardigan Railway |
| YTW | Ystalyfera Tin Works |

**Ex-War Department classes:**

| Class | Wheel Arrangement | Origin | Number in Class 1948 | 1961 |
|---|---|---|---|---|
| WD | 2-8-0 | WD | 499 | 730 |
| WD | 2-10-0 | WD | — | 23 |
| **Number of classes:** | | | *1 | 2 |
| **Number of locomotives:** | | | *499 | 753 |

*See also ex-LNER Class O7.

| Class | Wheel Arrangement | Origin | Number in Class 1948 | Number in Class 1961 |
|---|---|---|---|---|
| **British Railways Standard Classes:** | | | | |
| 9F | 2-10-0 | BR | — | 251 |
| 8P | 4-6-2 | BR | — | 1 |
| 7P6F 'Britannia' | 4-6-2 | BR | — | 55 |
| 6P5F 'Clan' | 4-6-2 | BR | — | 10 |
| 5MT | 4-6-0 | BR | — | 172 |
| 4MT | 4-6-0 | BR | — | 80 |
| 4MT | 2-6-0 | BR | — | 115 |
| 3MT | 2-6-0 | BR | — | 20 |
| 2MT | 2-6-0 | BR | — | 65 |
| 4MT | 2-6-4T | BR | — | 155 |
| 3MT | 2-6-0 | BR | — | 65 |
| 2MT | 2-6-2T | BR | — | 30 |
| **Number of classes:** | | | — | 12 |
| **Number of locomotives:** | | | — | 999 |

### SUMMARY

| Railway | Number of Classes 1948 | Number of Classes 1961 | Number of Locomotives 1948 | Number of Locomotives 1961 |
|---|---|---|---|---|
| LNER | 146 | 55 | 6,424 | 2,520 |
| LMS | 112 | 64 | 7,805 | 4,862 |
| SR | 87 | 39 | 1,810 | 782 |
| GWR | 73 | 32 | 3,777 | 2,499 |
| WD | 1 | 2 | 499 | 753 |
| BR | — | 12 | — | 999 |
| *Totals* | 419 | 204 | 20,315 | 12,415 |

| | 1948 | 1961 |
|---|---|---|
| **Average number of locomotives per class:** | 48.4 | 60.9 |

### Summary of Motive Power Depots 1950 and 1961

| Region | Number of depots 1950 | Number of depots 1961 |
|---|---|---|
| Eastern | 50 | 32 |
| North Eastern | 32 | 35 |
| London Midland | 119 | 93 |
| Scottish | 44 | 42 |
| Southern | 37 | 26 |
| Western | 62 | 60 |
| Total | 344 | 288 |

All the above were depots having an allocation of steam locomotives. The summary excludes sub-depots.

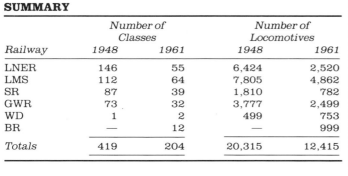

*Above:*
**The Great Eastern 'Claud Hamilton' 4-4-0s were good lookers. No 62548 was portrayed at March shed in April 1958.** *T. B. Owen/Colour-Rail BRE562*

*Top:*
**Ex-Great Central 'D11' 4-4-0 No 62663 *Prince Albert* leaves the now closed Sheffield Victoria station in September 1958 with a local service.** *P. J. Hughes/Colour-Rail BRE292*

The graceful lines of a Drummond 'Greyhound' are exemplified by 'T9' 4-4-0 No 30120 posing at Eastleigh depot in 1957. *Colour-Rail BRS22*

102

Even in the standardisation atmosphere of the 1950s some livery variations did appear. Otherwise this smart ex-Great Northern 0-6-0ST No 68846 (Class J52) would have been plain black. *W. Potter/Colour-Rail BRE409*

*Left:*

**The GWR 'Dukedogs' were basically 'Bulldog' chassis carrying 'Duke' type boilers. As such they were the last 4-4-0s to survive in Western Region service. No 9015 takes a local passenger train for Machynlleth near Llandre in August 1958.** *T. B. Owen/Colour-Rail BRW501*

*Left:*

**The Midland Railway's influence on the London, Tilbury & Southend Railway's locomotives is clear from this view of LTSR 4-4-2T No 41978 at Shoeburyness depot in 1956, near the end of its life.** *T. B. Owen/Colour-Rail BRM699*

*Below:*

**Designed specifically to negotiate the sharp curves at Southampton docks, Adams' 'B4' 0-4-0Ts of the LSWR were quite strong little machines. No 30083 poses at Eastleigh.** *Colour-Rail BRS4*

*Above:*
**The smallest ex-Great Western passenger tanks were the '14XX' class, of which No 1421 is pausing at Culmstock with the single coach 12.09pm to Tiverton Junction. This charming scene was photographed in November 1962.**
*P. W. Gray/Colour-Rail BRW452*

*Below:*
**An ex-North British Railway Class J83 0-6-0T, No 68474, tugs a few wagons into Edinburgh's Waverley station.**
*J. G. Wallace/Colour-Rail SC436*

*Above:*

**Small engines often had to work hard. The ex-SECR 'R1' class 0-6-0Ts which were used to haul and bank boat trains up the steep grade from Folkestone Harbour to the junction were flogged unmercifully on this duty. This one was pictured at Dover Priory shed in July 1959.** *Colin Boocock*

*Left:*

**Another group of ancient engines that worked hard right up to the end of their lives was the Midland '1F' 0-6-0T class which was hired to the ironworks at Staveley. No 41708 heads a mixed train of wagons in 1963.** *Colin Boocock*

*Left:*

**Aberdeen harbour was shunted by four small 0-4-2Ts from the former GNSR, like No 68192 which was still there in 1959, but had gone by the summer of 1960.**
*Don Beecroft/Colour-Rail SC445*

# 2 Dimensions of Principal Classes

| Class | Weight (tons) | Boiler pressure (lb/sq in) | Cylinders: number and size | Driving wheels | Tractive effort (lb/ft) |
|---|---|---|---|---|---|
| **8P** | | | | | |
| BR '8P' | 101 | 250 | (3) 18×28in | 6ft 2in | 39,080 |
| LM 'Coronation' | 105 | 250 | (4) 16.5×28in | 6ft 9in | 40,000 |
| LM 'Princess' | 104 | 250 | (4) 16.25×28in | 6ft 6in | 40,285 |
| ER 'A1' | 104 | 250 | (3) 19×26in | 6ft 8in | 37,400 |
| ER 'A4' | 102 | 250 | (3) 18.5×26in | 6ft 8in | 35,455 |
| SR Rebuilt 'Merchant Navy' | 98 | 250 | (3) 18×24in | 6ft 2in | 33,495 |
| WR 'King' | 89 | 250 | (4) 16.25×28in | 6ft 6in | 40,285 |
| **7P** | | | | | |
| BR '7MT' | 94 | 250 | (2) 20×28in | 6ft 2in | 32,150 |
| ER 'A3' | 96 | 220 | (3) 19×26in | 6ft 8in | 32,910 |
| SR 'WC'/'BB' | 86/90 | 250 | (3) 16.1×24in | 6ft 2in | 27,715 |
| ER 'V2' | 93 | 220 | (3) 18.5×26in | 6ft 2in | 33,730 |
| LM 'Royal Scot' | 93 | 250 | (3) 18×26in | 6ft 9in | 33,150 |
| WR 'Castle' | 80 | 225 | (4) 16×26in | 6ft 8.5in | 31,625 |
| SR 'Lord Nelson' | 84 | 220 | (4) 16.5×26in | 6ft 7in | 33,510 |
| **6P** | | | | | |
| BR 'Clan' | 87 | 225 | (2) 19.5×28in | 6ft 2in | 27,520 |
| LM 'Jubilee' | 80 | 225 | (3) 17×26in | 6ft 9in | 26,610 |
| WR 'County' | 77 | 250 | (2) 18.5×30in | 6ft 3in | 28,240 |
| **5MT** | | | | | |
| BR '5MT' | 76 | 225 | (2) 19×28in | 6ft 2in | 26,120 |
| LM '5MT' | 72/75 | 225 | (2) 18.5×28in | 6ft 0in | 25,455 |
| ER 'B1' | 71 | 225 | (2) 20×26in | 6ft 2in | 26,880 |
| SR 'N15' | 82 | 200 | (2) 20.5×28in | 6ft 7in | 25,320 |
| WR 'Hall' | 75/76 | 225 | (2) 18.5×30in | 6ft 0in | 27,275 |
| WR 'Grange' | 74 | 225 | (2) 18.5×30in | 5ft 8in | 28,875 |
| WR 'Manor' | 69 | 225 | (2) 18×30in | 5ft 8in | 27,340 |
| **4MT** | | | | | |
| BR 4-6-0 | 69 | 225 | (2) 18×28in | 5ft 8in | 25,100 |
| BR 2-6-0 | 59 | 225 | (2) 17.5×26in | 5ft 3in | 24,170 |
| LM 2-6-0 | 59 | 225 | (2) 17.5×26in | 5ft 3in | 24,170 |
| WR 43XX | 62/65 | 200 | (2) 18.5×30in | 5ft 8in | 25,670 |
| SR 'N' | 61 | 200 | (2) 19×28in | 5ft 6in | 26,035 |
| **4MT Tank** | | | | | |
| BR | 89 | 225 | (2) 18×28in | 5ft 8in | 25,100 |
| LM Fairburn | 85 | 200 | (2) 19.6×26in | 5ft 9in | 24.670 |
| ER 'L1' | 90 | 225 | (2) 20×26in | 5ft 2in | 32,080 |
| WR 61XX | 79 | 225 | (2) 18×30in | 5ft 8in | 27,340 |
| **8F/9F** | | | | | |
| BR '9F' | 87 | 250 | (2) 20×28in | 5ft 0in | 39,670 |
| WD 2-8-0 | 70 | 225 | (2) 19×28in | 4ft 8.5in | 34,215 |
| LM '8F' | 72 | 225 | (2) 18.5×28in | 4ft 8.5in | 32,440 |
| ER 'O1' | 73 | 225 | (2) 20×26in | 4ft 8in | 35,520 |
| WR 28XX | 76 | 225 | (2) 18.5×30in | 4ft 7.5in | 35,380 |
| **5F/4F** | | | | | |
| ER 'J39' | 58 | 180 | (2) 20×26in | 5ft 2in | 25,665 |
| SR 'Q1' | 51 | 230 | (2) 19×26in | 5ft 1in | 30,080 |
| LM '4F' | 49 | 175 | (2) 20×26in | 5ft 3in | 24,555 |
| **3MT** | | | | | |
| BR 2-6-0 | 57 | 200 | (2) 17.4×26in | 5ft 3in | 21,490 |
| WR 45XX | 57/61 | 200 | (2) 17×24in | 4ft 7.5in | 21,250 |
| WR 2251 | 43 | 200 | (2) 17.5×24in | 5ft 2in | 20,155 |
| **3MT Tank** | | | | | |
| BR 2-6-2T | 74 | 200 | (2) 17.5×26in | 5ft 3in | 21,490 |
| LM 2-6-2T | 71/73 | 200 | (2) 17.5×26in | 5ft 3in | 21,490 |
| **2MT** | | | | | |
| BR 2-6-0 | 49 | 200 | (2) 16.5×24in | 5ft 0in | 18,515 |
| LM 2-6-0 | 47 | 200 | (2) 16×24in | 5ft 0in | 17,410 |
| **2MT Tank** | | | | | |
| BR 2-6-2T | 63 | 200 | (2) 16.5×24in | 5ft 0in | 18,515 |
| LM 2-6-2T | 63 | 200 | (2) 16×24in | 5ft 0in | 17,410 |

At Polmadie depot, Glasgow, in September 1956 stands No 46118 *Royal Welch Fusilier* showing off the graceful form of the 'Rebuilt Scots'. *J. G. Wallace/Colour-rail SC338*

A nice clean '9F' shows off its bulk at South Pelaw while hauling coal hoppers for Consett in July 1966.
*J. G. Dewing/Colour-Rail BRE148*

*Top:*
**Near the top end of the dimensional scale were the LMS 'Princess Royal' 4-6-2s. No 46203 *Princess Margaret Rose* stands at Carlisle Citadel station between duties.**
*Colin Boocock*

*Above:*
**The LMS 'Jubilees' totalled 191 locomotives, of which No 45675 *Hardy*, seen here at Willesden depot, is a splendid example.** *Colin Boocock*

110

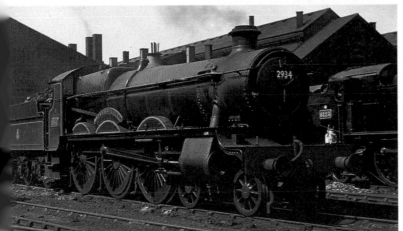

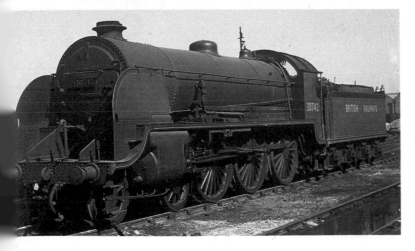

*Above:*
**No 31790 was one of the original SECR 2-6-4T 'River' class that had been rebuilt as Class U 2-6-0s by the Southern Railway following the Sevenoaks derailment. In July 1959 it was photographed at Tonbridge shortly after a works overhaul.** *Colin Boocock*

*Left:*
**In June 1950 one of the last GW 'Saint' 4-6-0s to be given an overhaul, No 2934 *Butleigh Court*, was photographed at Swindon shed.** *T. B. Owen/Colour-Rail BRW417*

*Left:*
**Urie 'Arthur' 4-6-0 No 30742 *Camelot* still carried SR malachite green livery at Eastleigh in 1950 though lettered and numbered by BR.** *T. B. Owen/Colour-Rail BRS389*

**Ribblehead Viaduct supports Class 5 No 44680 and its up freight, backed by snow-capped Whernside in April 1967.**
*D. Smith/Colour-Rail BRM722*

**With the morning sun having dispersed the majority of the overnight frost, Birmingham RC&W Class 33/0 No 33027 _Earl Mountbatten of Burma_ makes a most attractive picture hauling the 11.17 Milford Haven-Swansea train between Clynderwen and Whitland on 12 January 1985 and is about to pass under the Llandewi to Llanfallteg road.**
_Nigel Dykhoff_

# PART TWO
# THE DAWN OF A NEW ERA

The demise of the traditional British steam locomotive in regular revenue-earning service in 1968 caused many of us railway enthusiasts of the 1950s and 1960s ('trainspotters', if you must) to turn our backs on the excitement of 'real' railways in general.

Instead of continuing to appreciate the 'living' railway, and accepting the consequences of progress and modernisation, we retreated for the duration into our memories.

A lot of us found some solace in model railways (and there were a lot of us, as it became the nation's second-largest hobby – railway modellers outnumbered only by the anglers), when we realised they would provide us with the introverted and insulated-from-reality world we sought – that virtual never-never land of yesteryear, where the sun always shines on the gleaming paintwork of express locos hurtling off to the seaside, their trains packed with fresh-faced travellers on their way to bucket-and-spade holidays by the sea.

Was reality ever truthfully like this, or had we been seduced by ancient marketing campaigns for the Sunny South Special?

Needless to say, in model form few of our railways ever managed to sustain any hurtling schedules, extending as they did little more than a couple of hundred yards or so inland from the branch terminus at Sandy Bay or Walmington-on-Sea (rather like some Preserved railways, some cynic might say).

As well, we pored endlessly over illustrated books representing (in selectively-edited form, naturally) the finest points of the Steam era as we saw them, which had been cruelly snatched away from us by that horrid Dr. Beeching (upon whose grave we would no doubt still gladly dance).

Beeching was, in fact, long gone from BR before the last round-up and massacre of the steam loco, even though by 1968 his notorious Report had had the effect of closing down 4000 miles of our beloved Railway (including a fair number of those branch lines to the seaside).

But in 1968 we were mostly incapable of really objective thinking about the Modern Railway, and what its minimum standards should really be. In the railway of our fantasies, there was no scheduled stop at Social Reality Junction, to contemplate the living hell and low pay of an engine-cleaner raking out loco ash-pans. Shades of the Victorian chimney-sweep! How many armchair engine-drivers would care to have been a real-life fireman, shovelling several tons of coal per day?

So, as the last remnants of pre-nationalisation rolling stock followed the steam locos off to an appointment with the cutter's torch, the excitement of the emerging Modern Railway was largely missed, shrouded as it generally was in the sterile uniformity of Corporate Blue Livery (a colour which has been reviled almost as much as Telecom's later feeble attempt to foist Corporate Yellow on traditional telephone boxes).

But, down in the depot, something was undeniably stirring. . . . . . .

The High Speed Train, originally announced as a concept in 1969, became reality by 1973, and fully operational by 1976 (we'll draw a tactful veil over the sad and troubled history of the Advanced Passenger Train). Its arrival gave the world of railways one of its most potent symbols of all time, and Advertising and Marketing were quick to seize on the image of the 125mph Flying Banana cutting a swathe through the countryside.

Suddenly, rail travel was (almost) glamorous again – perhaps of no great interest to the car-owning masses and the new generation of children which had never ridden in a train, but at least rail-users could begin to feel less like objects of pity regarding their condition.

As a superb vindication, in 1978 the HST won a Design Council Award for "the high quality of its passenger comfort when travelling at speeds which cannot be sustained or bettered by any other form of fare-paying passenger land-vehicle".

Railways, having become in the eyes of the many 'modern-thinking' people an outmoded form of transport, could now boast (from 1071) a fully-computerised system for controlling and monitoring freight traffic, TOPS by name (Total Operations Processing System – unfortunately 20 years too late to recapture lost wagon-load traffic, but a step in the right direction nonetheless).

Electrification proceeded apace, with the West Coast Main Line north of Crewe to Glasgow authorised in 1970. Also, the image of urban transport was given a huge boost by the opening of the first section of the Tyne & Wear Metro in 1980.

In 1982, not a single passenger was killed in a railway accident. Although that image of safety has been rather nullified in recent times by the likes of the Clapham Junction Disaster, there has been a developing awareness that the style of construction of modern trains makes them safer. By jettisoning old-style railway construction methods, there was an added advantage in design terms of making trains more closely resemble the products of the Automotive Industry, i.e. members of the car-owning democracy would feel themselves less in alien surroundings, as compared to their normal standards of comfort, when travelling by train.

Another exciting visual concept helping to chase away boring uniformity was the introduction of Business Sectors in 1982, moving the responsibility for marketing and finance from the five regions. This facilitated an explosion of new liveries to differentiate between Inter City, Provincial, Network South East,

Railfreight and Parcels, and there was burgeoning local independence shown by various Passenger Transport Executives with local trains taking on some very non-traditional colours like orange and pale blue. Passengers could begin to feel some identification with trains of their area or region, and a sense of their railway not being totally subject to BRB Headquarters' diktat.

And then came the 'Sprinter', a DMU every bit comparable to the ones everyone envied on trips abroad, intended as a replacement for the huge fleet of ancient 'rattlers' on country branch and Provincial services. With power-operated 'plug' doors, lavatories and public address systems on these trains, the future was looking good even for non-prestige routes.

Stations re-opened, new stations, Mk.IV carriages, Networkers, Wessex Expresses . . . . . . . one could go on and on. The future looks exciting for railways. Who could say the same about Road Transport?

It's time to be interested in railways again!!!!

**The much-loved 'Deltics' were the most powerful passenger diesel locomotives on BR, at 3,300bhp, and for almost 20 years dominated East Coast main line passenger services. No 55013 *The Black Watch* powers up Beattock Bank with a diverted King's Cross-Edinburgh train on 4 May 1980.** *D. Rogers*

116

A Class 254 InterCity 125 led by power car No 43065 races through Pilmoor on 9 August 1986, forming the 13.00 King's Cross-Aberdeen service. *John E. Oxley*

# TEN

# INTERCITY AND INTER-REGIONAL

British Rail's InterCity network radiates from Paddington to Bristol, Wales and the West Country; from Euston to Birmingham, Manchester, Liverpool, Glasgow and Inverness; from King's Cross to Hull, Leeds, Newcastle, Edinburgh and Aberdeen; from St Pancras to Nottingham, Derby and Sheffield; from Liverpool Street to East Anglia, and also incorporates North-east/South-west route trains via both Birmingham New Street and Kensington Olympia in London. With the exception of trains from Euston, some from Paddington and Liverpool Street and the cross-London services, motive power is usually entrusted to the InterCity 125 High Speed Trains. Electric locomotives, primarily of Classes 86 and 87, work the West Coast main line expresses and Class 86s some of the Liverpool Street ones. Class 47s still appear on some InterCity services from Liverpool Street and Paddington and Class 50s operate extensively on the Western Region, in particular west of Plymouth.

The Inter-Regional cross-country services via Birmingham also utilise some InterCity 125 sets but most of this traffic is still locomotive-hauled, with Classes 47 and 50 now dominating following the withdrawal of large numbers of the Class 45 'Peaks'. The requirement for passengers to change trains on long journeys is very much reduced with through services from Aberdeen and Glasgow to the West Country; from Dundee and Glasgow to Poole; from Liverpool, Manchester, Derby and Wolverhampton to Brighton; from Cardiff to Newcastle; from Liverpool and Manchester to Plymouth and Dover and many more.

*Below:*
**Reflected in the still waters of the Kennet & Avon Canal, near Crofton, a Class 253 HST set, with power car No 43174 leading, heads eastwards along the Berks & Hants route, forming the 07.25 Penzance-Paddington express on 16 June 1984.** *John Vaughan*

*Top:*
**Passing the disused signalbox which marks the site of the once busy Brent station in South Devon, Class 50 No 50049 *Defiance* powers the 13.40 Paddington-Penzance towards Plymouth on 16 July 1985.** *Brian Morrison*

*Above:*
**Having arrived with the 08.02 from Glasgow Central, Class 370 Advanced Passenger Train formation No 370007 rests alongside newly-named Class 86/2 electric locomotive No 86245 *Dudley Castle* on the 13.40 to Wolverhampton at Euston on 17 August 1984.** *Brian Morrison*

*Right:*
**With power car number 43187 neatly lettered on the drawbar cover plate, a Class 253 HST set passes Ambergate on 6 July 1985 forming the 16.00 Sheffield-St Pancras service.** *Les Nixon*

*Right:*
**When this photograph was taken on 6 July 1979, some two years were to elapse before the revised Class 50 fleet livery of wrap-round yellow ends, black window surrounds, grey roof panels together with large BR logo and TOPS number was to emerge from the BREL Works at Doncaster. In original, albeit work-stained livery, No 50023** *Howe* **passes the time-worn but classic setting of Horse Cove, near Dawlish, heading the 11.30 Paddington-Penzance, the renowned 'Cornish Riviera' express.**
*Brian Morrison*

*Below:*
**On 15 August 1986, the 16.45 Euston-Blackpool North 'Lancashire Pullman' approaches Watford Junction headed by Class 86/2 No 86227** *Sir Henry Johnson.*
*John E. Oxley*

**Top:**
With semaphore signals still extant, Class 47/4 No 47480 *Robin Hood* enters Wellington station on 10 June 1985 rostered to the 11.40 Shrewsbury-Euston service. An electric locomotive will take over from the 'Duff' at Wolverhampton for the remainder of the journey under the wires to London.  *Brian J. Robbins*

**Above:**
Class 50 No 50037 *Illustrious* leaves Cheltenham on the bitterly cold 15 February 1985 with the 09.36 Liverpool Lime Street-Penzance service.  *Peter W. Durham*

**Right:**
With the early morning sun soon to be obliterated by the storm clouds rolling in from the west, a Class 253 HST set, led by power car No 43124, approaches Taunton station on 28 March 1985 forming the 07.25 express from Plymouth to Paddington.  *Colin J. Marsden*

*Left:*
In immaculate InterCity red and grey livery on the day that the locomotive was named *University of London* by Her Royal Highness Princess Anne at Euston station, No 86434 prepares to move away from Euston with the 14.05 for Birmingham New Street on 10 April 1986.   *Brian Morrison*

*Below:*
On 29 May 1985, the down 'Manchester Pullman' races past Slindon, north of Norton Bridge in Staffordshire, hauled by Class 86/1 No 86102 *Robert A. Riddles*. This electric locomotive is just one of a sub-class of three rebuilt with Class 87-type bogies and motors for evaluation of equipment, prior to its installation in the Class 87 fleet.
*Hugh Ballantyne*

*Bottom:*
Class 45/1 'Peak' No 45139 is rostered for the 07.50 Bristol Temple Meads-Penzance service on 5 July 1984 and restarts the train from the scheduled Lostwithiel stop. The line in the foreground is the start of the old Fowey branch, now used for china clay traffic to and from Carne Point.
*Brian Morrison*

*Above:*
**The time-honoured Liverpool Street setting where everything from early steam engines through to the 'Britannia' Pacifics and, latterly, Class 37 and 47 diesels have been photographed. Now it is the turn of the electric locomotives, with Class 86/2 No 86221 *Vesta* awaiting departure time with the 13.30 to Norwich on 29 May 1985.**
*Roger Norman*

*Below:*
**Near Glenmuckloch Hall, between New Cumnock and Kirkconnel, on 6 July 1985, Class 47/4 No 47403 *The Geordie* growls past hauling the Saturdays 11.00 Ayr-Euston service. Note the Gateshead depot sticker between the marker lights.** *Peter J. Robinson*

*Above:*
**Named Class 254 InterCity 125 power car No 43100 *Craigentinny* leads an immaculate eight-car formation at Plawsworth, Co Durham, on 1 May 1986 forming the 13.35 Edinburgh-King's Cross express.** *Peter J. Robinson*

*Right:*
**A scene from the late 1970s as a Class 46 1Co-Co1 No 46043 nears Batley hauling the 07.42 inter-regional service from Newcastle to Liverpool Lime Street.** *Gavin Morrison*

# ELEVEN

# LONDON & SOUTH EAST AND PROVINCIAL

Whilst the High Speed Trains operating the prestigious InterCity services provide most of British Rail's glamour, and are the focus for the majority of their media marketing, it is still the much maligned, taken for granted, traditional train that makes up the largest proportion of timetabled services.

The Network SouthEast area embraces the whole of the Southern Region passenger network and also includes the suburban trains that emanate from the London termini of the Eastern, London Midland and Western Regions. Other than non-passenger workings, the Provincial Sector covers just about everything else and stretches from Wick and Thurso, on the northerly tip of Scotland, to the furthest extremity of Cornwall at Penzance.

*Below:*
**The 09.00 Exeter St Davids-Exmouth local working departs from Exeter Central on 23 July 1985 formed of a Birmingham RC&W Suburban 3-car Class 118 DMU, led by motor brake second No W51303. Observe the colourful graffiti adorning the brickwork of the old signalbox in lieu of the nameplate.** *Brian Morrison*

*Left:*
**Class 37 Co-Co No 37237 makes a rousing start from Carlisle with the 14.30 summer Saturdays only Morecambe-Glasgow Central train on a very wet August day in 1978. If the weather in Morecambe was the same as in Carlisle, the returning holidaymakers will be glad to have gone home!** *Antony Guppy*

*Below:*
**A Cravens Class 105 2-car DMU with driving trailer composite No E54447 leading approaches Spital Bridge, Peterborough, on 24 April 1985 forming the 15.15 service from Birmingham New Street to Cambridge, a journey time of over 3½ hours.** *Bill Sharman*

*Right:*
**Resplendent in freshly applied ScotRail livery, Class 47/7 No 47701 *Saint Andrew* leads Class 33/0 No 33035 on the 11.15 Crewe-Bangor train on 19 March 1986 and passes the battlements of the magnificent Conwy Castle. The leading machine is probably on a running-in turn following overhaul at Crewe Works.** *Larry Goddard*

*Left:*
**With Class 37s having taken over from the Class 25s on the Cambrian lines from 1985, Nos 37227 and 37220 leave Shrewsbury behind on 18 August 1985 hauling the 07.30 Euston-Aberystwyth summer Saturdays train.**
*Brian J. Robbins*

*Below left:*
**Class 205/1 diesel electric multiple-unit No 1111 was selected for extensive refurbishing during 1979 and emerged from Eastleigh Works in 1980 with gangways fitted, compartments replaced by open seating layout, fluorescent lighting and a public address system. The 3-car unit has since been used extensively on the Ashford-Hastings route where it was photographed on 13 April 1985 arriving at Appledore, Kent, as the 16.40 ex-Ashford.**
*Brian Morrison*

*Left:*
**A bird's-eye view of Lostwithiel from the hills above the Cornish town. On the evening of 5 July 1984, the 16.35 stopping train from Plymouth to Penzance winds away from the station hauled by Class 50 No 50010 *Monarch*.** *Brian Morrison*

*Right:*
**Standing at Inverness on 15 November 1984 with the 10.55 for Kyle of Lochalsh, Class 37 No 37260 *Radio Highland* brightens a drab day in the Highland capital. The aerial on the loco bonnet (above the headlight) is used in connection with the radio electronic token block equipment system.**
*Colin J. Marsden*

*Above:*
**A slight delay in departure of the 12.25 local service to Morpeth was fortuitous for the photographer on 29 May 1980 when the 12.30 for South Shields left at the same time and brought about this well-positioned view which also includes Class 31/1 No 31139 working light engine. The two Cravens Class 105 2-car DMUs are led by driving trailer composites Nos E56426 and E56459 (latterly Nos 54426 and 54459) and the scene is, of course, the well known one from above Newcastle station.** *Brian Morrison*

*Right:*
**A Class 101 Metro-Cammell 2-car DMU, led by driving trailer second No E54071, forms the 10.15 Newcastle-Middlesbrough service at Stockton on 20 August 1984.**
*Bill Sharman*

*Top:*
**Although Four Oaks station lies on the cross-city route from Redditch to Lichfield City, via Birmingham New Street, a number of the services in fact terminate there, resulting in the sidings being used as a stabling point for a number of DMUs. Awaiting their next scheduled duty on 1 March 1984 are two BR Derby-built Class 116 units with the motor brake second cars Nos M53852 and M53062 facing the camera.** *Brian Morrison*

*Above:*
**On 6 July 1985 the local passenger service from Tunbridge Wells Central to Eridge via Tunbridge Wells West and Groombridge was withdrawn. Trains were generally formed of St Leonards-based Class 207 diesel electric multiple-units (DEMUs) such as No 1305 pictured here at the impressive Tunbridge Wells West station on 24 April 1985 as the 14.47 from Eridge to Tunbridge Wells Central.** *Brian Morrison*

*Right:*
**A journey time of over 4½ hours would be in prospect for anyone contemplating travelling the whole route of the 14.20 from Crewe to Cleethorpes. A few passengers alight from the train at Spondon but they have only made a six minute trip from Derby in the Swindon Class 120 3-car DMU No 509. Motor brake second No M53657 is the car nearest to the camera.** *Brian Morrison*

BR Derby Class 116 DMU No C335, with motor brake second No W51140 leading, leaves Abercynon on 29 August 1985 forming a Merthyr Tydfil-Cardiff Central train. Note the Welsh Dragon embellishment below the centre cab window. *Les Nixon*

C 335

*Above left:*
With the West Midlands PTE logo prominent on the yellow front, a Class 116 Derby-built DMU, with motor brake second No M53055 leading, leaves Shrewsbury on 6 July 1985 forming the 08.20 to Wolverhampton. On the right, Class 37 No 37294 waits for the road with the delayed 07.53 for Aberystwyth, having arrived earlier as empty coaching stock from Bescot. *John Vaughan*

*Left:*
A particularly attractive scene at Lincoln on 21 August 1984 with swans in the foreground and the cathedral in the background. A BR Swindon Class 120 Cross-Country DMU makes the crossing of the River Witham at Lincoln St Marks. *Bill Sharman*

*Top:*
Transferred from the Cardiff 'Valley Lines' allocation to Plymouth Laira to work Cornish branch lines, Pressed Steel Co Class 121 single car 'Bubble' No 55033 still retains the Welsh Dragon emblem at Liskeard on 1 October 1985 whilst working the Looe branch. *Brian Morrison*

*Above:*
The slab-sided design of the Class 201/202/203 'Hastings' DEMUs was necessary in view of the restricted tunnels on the Hastings route from Tonbridge. It was unusual for these types to operate anywhere other than on the Charing Cross/Cannon Street-Hastings route and in this view Class 201 unit No 1003 approaches Stonegate station on 21 March 1986 forming the 11.45 Charing Cross-Hastings. With the tunnel problems alleviated, the 29-year reign of these units came to an end when the Queen Mother inaugurated the new route electrification that came into full use on 6 May 1986. *Brian Morrison*

*Above:*
**Class 150/1 'Sprinter' unit No 150136 calls at Lowdham station on 10 February 1986, forming the 12.32 Lincoln-Crewe train.**
*E. A. J. Saunders*

*Right:*
**With the VSOE Pullman set in tow for a special running to Northfleet in Kent on 6 September 1985, Class 73/1 electro-diesel No 73112 passes Charlton station, in southeast London.**
*Brian Morrison*

# TWELVE

# THE FREIGHT SCENE

During the past few years British Rail's freight business has undergone a quiet revolution, both in operational and management techniques. Traditional, but unremunerative, vacuum-braked or partially fitted mixed loads linking labour-intensive marshalling yards are nearly a thing of the past, although the virtual demise of this type of operation has not necessarily resulted in the business being lost to road transport, as a considerable amount has gone over to the Railfreight Sector's fast-growing Speedlink services which are also attracting many new customers.

Coal and coke merry-go-round trains make up almost half of BR's freight income, with the remainder resulting from significant contributions from the movement of aggregates, cement, steel, oil, grain, chemicals, bricks, motor vehicles and refuse etc. In addition, van traffic caters for the carriage of newspapers, parcels and some remaining perishables and, of course, there is also the vital role of both Freightliner Ltd and the block workings involving privately-owned wagons.

Locomotive power ranges from the 204bhp of the Class 03s to the 3,300bhp of the Class 58s, with almost every current class of BR locomotive being utilised in some way or another.

*Below:*
**Crewe-built Class 56 Co-Co No 56131 passes Low Fell on 20 June 1985 hauling loaded Merry-go-round hoppers from Swalwell Colliery to Tyne yard for distribution.**
*Peter J. Robinson*

*Above:*

**A brace of InterCity-liveried Class 87/0 electric locomotives, with No 87003 *Patriot* leading No 87006 *City of Glasgow* on a Willesden-Glasgow Gushetfaulds Freightliner service, pictured in the Lune Valley on 28 June 1986. Note the differing forms of this livery carried by the two locomotives.** *Peter J. Robinson*

*Below:*

**The Class 58 Co-Co fleet of locomotives represent dedicated power for Railfreight's most important traffic. On 18 February 1985 No 58024 hauls an up coal-laden MGR** train along the Erewash Valley line at Bennerley, Ilkeston. The disused viaduct in the background once carried Great Northern Railway tracks to Derby Friargate.
*Colin J. Marsden*

*Bottom:*

**It isn't often that a Class 31 A1A-A1A is given charge of a rake of MGR wagons, or that such a train should have a brakevan! All is not as it seems, however, as No 31139 comes off the former Midland Railway line through Castle Donnington and joins the main Derby-Burton/Crewe route at Stenson Junction on 1 July 1983; the train is heading northwards for the hoppers to be serviced.** *Brian Morrison*

*Top:*
**With a long haul of ARC hoppers, Class 56 No 56047 is held in a Westbury siding on the evening of 31 August 1984 and will proceed westwards on the following morning.**
*Brian Morrison*

*Above:*
**A locomotive class other than 47, 37, 31 or 08 at Ripple Lane yards, Barking, is somewhat unusual and for a Class 33 to be in attendance on oil tanks is extremely rare. On 23 September 1985, No 33038 heads back to Furzebrook oil terminal and more familiar Southern Region metals.**
*Brian Morrison*

*Left:*
**A Class 37 cautiously winds its load of chemical tanks across the pointwork at the north of Newcastle station on 29 May 1980.** *Brian Morrison*

*Below:*
**Class 20 Bo-Bo locomotives Nos 20077 and 20141 round the curve at Buxworth with empty 'Peakstone' hoppers from Northwich, returning to one of the Peak District quarries on 30 May 1985.** *Ian Gould*

*Right:*
**On 3 April 1985, Class 56 No 56075 heads south at Besborough, between Market Harborough and Kettering, with a Tarmac stone train.** *Bill Sharman*

*Below right:*
**Class 56 locomotives Nos 56039 and 56088 leave Llanwern on 19 May 1986 with a train of empty hoppers for Port Talbot.** *Mike Jones*

*Left:*
**Fly-ash wagons from Ratcliffe-on-Soar power station to the CEGB Fletton tip pass Sutton Bonington, on the Midland main line, on 27 June 1983 with motive power provided by Class 56 No 56098. Why someone has felt obliged to scrawl the last three digits of the TOPS number in very amateurish fashion below the air-horn covers is not known.**
*Brian Morrison*

*Below left:*
**Disparate liveried Class 73/1 electro-diesels Nos 73132 and 73141 work in multiple on 19 April 1985 at Tolworth, Surrey, with a Hall Aggregates train from Newhaven stone terminal.** *Colin J. Marsden*

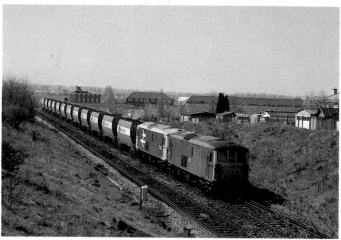

*Below:*
**The attractive livery applied to Class 73/1 No 73102 *Air Tour Suisse* for the 'Gatwick Express' services looks a little incongruous when the locomotive is rostered for a freight turn. On 13 July 1985 a rake of Rugby Cement wagons at St Denys, near Southampton, heads for Halling cement works in Kent via Hoo Junction, having emanated from Bevois Park.** *John Vaughan*

*Right:*
**The four General Motors locomotives constructed in the USA for Foster Yeoman commenced working a number of stone trains from Merehead Quarry in February 1986. Owned and operated exclusively by Foster Yeoman, they are the first private-owner locomotives to be allowed to work on BR main lines; albeit with BR drivers. Incorporating transport of stone with driver training, No 59002 *Yeoman Enterprise* is seen on the Purfleet-Merehead empties at Ealing Broadway on 15 August 1986.**
*John E. Oxley*

*Above:*
**Class 20 No 20163, in Railfreight livery, heads a permanent way train at Nuneaton on 7 May 1986.** *Chris Milner*

*Above:*
**Nicely lined-out 'Peak' Class 45/0 No 45013 passes Dudley signalbox, on the freight-only line from Stourbridge Junction to Pleck Junction, Walsall, with an ABS freight for Bescot on 3 June 1985.** *Brian J. Robbins*

*Below:*
**On 1 July 1985 an ABS from Scunthorpe to Craiginches Yard, Aberdeen, consists primarily of Grainflow Polybulks and steel-carrying wagons as Class 37 No 37006 takes the load through Stone Bridge, Durham. Note the two headlights fitted to the locomotive in place of the usual boxed marker lights.** *Peter J. Robinson*

*Below:*

**A St Blazey-Goonbarrow ABS composed of two English China Clay bogie hoppers leased from Tiger Rail Ltd and two Cargowaggons heads down the Newquay branch at Luxulyan on 3 October powered by Cornish Railways Class 37 No 37207 *William Cookworthy*.** *Brian Morrison*

*Below right:*

**An early morning haul of clay hoods from Moorswater Dries for unloading at Carne Point, runs along the freight only section of line from Moorswater to Coombe Junction on 2 October 1985 hauled by Class 37 No 37247. The 1,750bhp**

**'Siphons' are permitted to haul 22 loaded clay hoods up the gradient to Liskeard and this view appears to be of a maximum loading.** *Brian Morrison*

*Bottom:*

**Class 37s No 37222 and Cornish Railways No 37196 *Tre Pol and Pen*, known locally as 'the twins', shunt china clay hoods at Parkandillack Dries on the same day. These wagons are now used only on local trip workings, to and from the various dries and Carne Point, with the PBA 'Tigers' taking over for the ABS services to the Potteries.** *Brian Morrison*

*Right:*
**Class 47/0 No 47098, of Crewe diesel depot, passes West Ealing on 3 August 1985 hauling the Saturday Ripple Lane-Southampton Maritime Freightliner.**
*John Vaughan*

*Below right:*
**A long haul of covered 'Cartics' bypass Crewe on the 'independent lines' on 3 July 1985 headed by Class 85 Bo-Bo electric No 85005. The train is the Ford Motor Co 12.27 Garston-Dagenham Dock.**
*John Vaughan*

*Below:*
**With the last snow of the winter proving reluctant to disappear, Class 37 No 37092 snarls up Belstead Bank, near Ipswich, on 16 February 1985 with a heavy ABS freight that includes open 'Cartics' for Mossend from Parkeston Quay.** *Michael J. Collins*

*Above:*
**A Tinsley-allocated Class 37, No 37125, heads a Sheffield-London parcels train between the tunnels at Welwyn, Hertfordshire, on 19 August 1978.**
*Antony Guppy*

*Right:*
**Class 73/1 electro-diesel No 73120 runs between New Malden and Raynes Park on 6 March 1985 hauling the 08.45 empty vans from Eastleigh to Clapham Junction yard.**
*Colin J. Marsden*

*Above:*
**A haul of steel coil from British Steel, Lackenby to British Steel, Corby passes Clay Cross, Derbyshire, on 6 March 1985 powered by snowplough-fitted Class 37 No 37096 working in multiple with sister locomotive No 37042. Both locomotives are a part of the Thornaby allocation.**
*Bert Wynn*

*Below:*
**Looking very smart in newly applied Railfreight Sector grey paint, Class 31/1 No 31160 backs its freight train into a siding at Eastfield signalbox, Peterborough, having arrived from the south on 7 March 1986.** *Bill Sharman*

*Right:*
**At many sidings can be found brake vans of various types gently rotting away; the advent of air-braked services and the demise of unfitted and partially-fitted mixed freights having led to their virtual disappearance from use on BR. On 3 April 1980, No 40143 hauls a train of empty mineral wagons on a Sandhills-Penmaenmawr working past Olive Mount.** *J. S. Buckley*

*Below right:*
**Class 31/1 No 31139 leaves Newcastle with a down train of empty wagons on 29 May 1980.** *Brian Morrison*

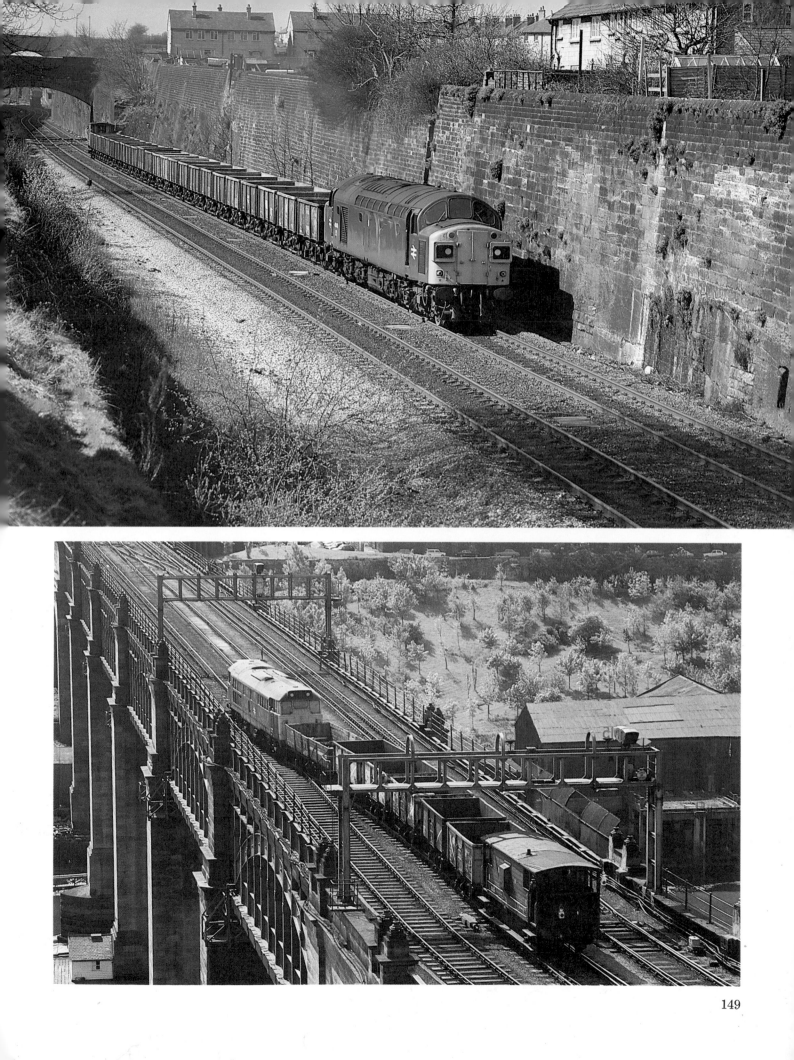

*Above:*
**The 10.36 driver-training special from Hither Green to the Kent Coast approaches Swanley, Kent, on 6 September 1985. Class 415/2 4-EPB EMUs Nos 5355 and 5310 are being hauled by Class 56 No 56047.** *Brian Morrison*

*Right:*
**Having completed the re-railment of a recalcitrant Class 415/1 EMU that formed the 09.02 Dartford-Charing Cross via Eltham train, the Hither Green breakdown train, including Rapier steam crane No ADRR95209, prepares to return home from Dartford on 8 January 1985 hauled by BRC&W Class 33/0 No 33047.** *Brian Morrison*

# THIRTEEN

# ON DEPOT

In the steam days of the 1950s there were some 332 engine sheds with a locomotive allocation, and very many more if the various sub-sheds were included. Today just 90 depots have a motive power allocation with another 31 listed as stabling or fuelling points. Many famous names from the past still exist, such as Old Oak Common, Bristol Bath Road, Willesden, Crewe, Carlisle, Newton Heath, Stratford, Norwich, York, Gateshead, Inverness, Eastfield, Stewarts Lane and Eastleigh. Many more, however, are merely names from an old Ian Allan *abc*. Camden, Rugby, New England, 'Top Link' King's Cross, Kittybrewster, St Margarets, Nine Elms and Exmouth Junction have all gone.

The smells are different today, the buildings are, for the most part, of modern and functional design and maintenance techniques are advanced to the extent that diesel and electric traction leaves far less work residue. One thing that remains, however, is the indefinable atmosphere. Whether it is a steam shed or a maintenance depot, that at least is still with us.

*Below:*
**On 8 May 1984, Class 87/0 Bo-Bo electric locomotive No 87012 *Coeur de Lion* peers out of Willesden Depot awaiting a media audience before officially unveiling the new InterCity 'Executive' livery in which it had been repainted.** *Brian Morrison*

*Above:*
**The colourful scene at Glasgow Eastfield on 12 June 1985. Apart from the standard liveried locomotives of Classes 08, 27 and 37, the visual highpoint consists of the Class 37 'Highland Terriers' Nos 37043 *Loch Lomond*, 37081 *Loch Long* and 37191 *International Youth Year 1985*.** *Tom Noble*

*Left:*
**Class 31/4 A1A-A1A No 31404, with white body stripe, stands in Bounds Green depot on 26 July 1979 with a train of Mk 1 stock which is being cleaned prior to use.** *Brian Morrison*

*Right:*
**With closure imminent, Westhouses depot has clearly seen better days as Class 20 No 20163 pauses between duties on the Erewash Valley freights on a dull 29 June 1983.** *Brian Morrison*

*Above:*

**A colourful line-up inside Old Oak Common depot for the 1985 Open Day with restored Class 35 'Hymek' No D7018 in original green livery, preserved Class 52 'Western' No D1015 *Western Champion* in golden ochre livery, together with Class 50 No 50007 *Sir Edward Elgar* and Class 47/4 No 47500 *Great Western* both in GWR green as a part of the GWR150 activities.** *Colin J. Marsden*

*Left:*

**Re-fuelling completed, Class 33/1 No 33103 waits to take the short journey from Stewarts Lane depot to Waterloo station on 12 October 1985 in order to power the 14.10 Waterloo-Salisbury train** *Brian Morrison*

*Above right:*

**At Cardiff Canton's Open Day on 6 July 1985, two of the special exhibits were Class 58 Co-Co No 58003 and Derby RTC Bo-Bo No 97201 *Experiment* (ex-Class 24 No 24061).** *Colin J. Marsden*

*Right:*

**Class 37 No 37104 receives attention inside Thornaby depot on 18 May 1982 alongside a Class 08 shunter and a Class 47.** *Stephen Montgomery*

*Above:*
**In sub-zero conditions it is common practice to keep engines ticking over in order to avoid any freeze-up. This is the case in this view at Bescot depot, including Class 45/0s Nos 45046, 45005 and 45069, with Class 56 No 56090 at the rear.** *Malcolm Inger*

*Right:*
**If one really tries, trains can be found in peculiar places! On 18 June 1984 Class 415/2 4-EPB EMU No 5364 is actually stabled in a siding at Blackfriars station awaiting the next turn of duty as part of the evening commuter services.**
*Brian Morrison*

# FOURTEEN

# TODAY'S MOTIVE POWER – OLD AND NEW

Of the locomotive class numbers allocated for the purposes of TOPS, ranging originally from 01 to 55, only 15 main types remain in service today plus three new varieties, Classes 56, 58 and 59. This rather bald statement, however, does not take into account the large number of variants within some of the types — and the consequent sub-classes created — and the interest in locomotives remains as high as ever. The majority of the representative classes of DMU, DEMU and EMU are also featured in this section with due emphasis being given to the older types being phased out and the newcomers that are making those older types look even older!

*Below:*

**The Class 305 EMU fleet was constructed from 1960 for use on the Liverpool Street suburban services. The blue and grey livery now applied has improved their appearance and some now sport a 'Jazz Train' motif between the cab windows as with this example, No 305408, passing Stratford on 3 September 1984 coupled to 305417 with ecs for Liverpool Street.** *Brian Morrison*

*Bottom:*

**The Class 307s were introduced in 1956 for use on the Great Eastern outer-suburban lines. All are 4-car sets allocated to Ilford. On 3 September 1984 No 307128 heads away from Stratford yards and makes for Liverpool Street with ecs to form a train for Shenfield.** *Brian Morrison*

15

*Above:*
On the same day, Class 309/2 express EMU No 309616 uses the up fast line at Stratford and leads unit No 309612 on a Clacton-Liverpool Street train. These types were introduced in 1961 and built at BR York expressly for the Clacton and Walton services, on which they still operate with distinction up to the present time. *Brian Morrison*

*Below:*
The first batch of new generation EMU stock emerged from BREL York in 1976 for use on the Great Northern inner-suburban area. These 64 3-car sets, designated Class 313, were followed in 1979 by a further batch of 16 high density units for the Glasgow Suburban lines classified 314. Unit No 314213 is seen at Partick on 31 May 1983 forming a Glasgow Central-Milngavie service and lettered 'Trans-Clyde'. *Les Nixon*

*Above:*

**Apart from the distinctive 'Strathclyde Transport' livery and the pantograph, the new Class 318 EMUs constructed at BREL Derby and York could be mistaken for a Southern Region Class 455/9. Twenty-one of these units came into use on Ayrshire line services in September 1986 and the first of them, No 318250, was previewed for the media on 6 June 1986 and is pictured here at Glasgow Central after working as a special to and from Lanark.** *Stuart Marshall*

*Above right:*

**The Class 411 4-CEP 'Kent Coasters' have been the basic power for the Kent Coast electrified system for more than 30 years, having been constructed at Eastleigh Works from 1955. The complete fleet was given extensive refurbishment at Swindon Works between 1976 and 1984 to include aluminium framed tinted glass windows, new design seats, lowered ceilings and fluorescent lighting. On 6 September 1985, unit No 1579 leads a Class 423 4-VEP No 7892 at Gillingham, Kent, forming the 11.52 train from London Victoria to Dover Priory via Herne Hill and Canterbury East.** *Brian Morrison*

*Right:*

**The first of the 213 Class 415 4-EPB EMUs emerged from Eastleigh in 1951; a more modern version of the Southern Railway's 4-SUB fleet with electro-pneumatic brakes and buck-eye couplings. During the period 1974-84 just under a quarter of them were 'facelifted' and re-classified as 415/4. On 14 August 1985, Class 415/1 No 5123 leaves Waterloo East making up the rear of the 15.08 Charing Cross-Orpington local service whilst Class 415/4 No 5461 arrives as the 14.20 Reigate-Charing Cross.** *Brian Morrison*

*Top:*
The approaches to Waterloo in May 1984 with, from left to right, Class 491 4-car trailer control unit No 429 leading a Bournemouth semi-fast, Class 421/2 4-CIG No 7344 at the head of a fast service for Portsmouth Harbour and Class 423 4-VEP No 7747 at the rear of an arrival. The 28 Class 491 4-TCs were constructed at York from 1966 for use with the 4-REP units on the electrified Bournemouth line. The 138 4-CIGs were built at York in three batches from 1964 to 1970 and were utilised on the Brighton, Portsmouth and Guildford/Reading services and replaced the old 4-COR series. All 194 of the 4-car high density 4-VEPs were also built at York from 1967 and operate throughout the Southern Region electrified system. *Brian Morrison*

*Above:*
The Class 420 4-BIGs were first introduced in 1965 when 18 4-car buffet units were built at York for use with the 4-CIGs on the Victoria-Brighton and South Coast lines with a further batch of 10 following in 1970 for the Waterloo-Portsmouth services. Now classified as 422/1, No 2101 passes Streatham North Junction on 30 May 1985 leading the 11.50 Victoria-Ore and is passed in the opposite direction by the 10.30 Hastings-Victoria with a Class 421/2 No 7399 bringing up the rear. *Colin J. Marsden*

*Left:*
Constructed at Eastleigh in 1957/58 for the Euston-Watford and Broad Street-Richmond services, the 57 three-car Class 501 EMUs have now been phased out and replaced by Southern Region Class 416/3 2-EPBs. During their last days, on 18 September 1985, No 501142 arrives at Euston from Watford Junction. *Brian J. Robbins*

*Below left:*
Motive power for the Isle of Wight system is provided by former London Transport underground stock, which even retains the clerestory roofs of the period in which it was manufactured — the late 1920s! As the island loading gauge is smaller than that on the mainland, this stock was purchased from London Transport rather than go to the expense of heightening most of the system's bridges in order to run modern standard stock. Before the stock was painted blue and white, the Ryde Pier Head-Ryde Esplanade shuttle crosses the pier over the Solent headed by Class 486 3-TIS unit No 031. *M. Pope*

*Below:*
The Southern Region's new generation 4-car EMU, the Class 455, began to appear from BREL York in 1982, mainly for use on the suburban network radiating from Waterloo. They replaced the Class 508s which had been used on the Southern Region as an interim measure prior to being transferred to Merseyside to replace the life-expired Class 503s. On 10 June 1986, Class 455/9 No 5908 waits to leave Waterloo with a Dorking service whilst Network SouthEast liveried Class 455/8 No 5872 forms a special in connection with the Sector's media launch of that day. Note the much cleaner front end arrangement of the newer unit. *Brian Morrison*

*Right:*

Three of the four cars that made up Class 508 EMU No 508016 now operate on Merseyside as unit No 508116. During their sojourn on Southern Region metals, the 09.05 from Chessington South arrives at Waterloo station on 22 October 1983. *R. S. Freeman*

*Below right:*

The most modern of the Southern Region's fleet of DEMUs are the 19 3-car sets that make up Class 207 introduced from Eastleigh in 1962 for use on the SR's non-electrified lines but, specifically, on the Oxted services. On 10 August 1985, No 1304 passes the unusual split distant signal near Birchden Junction whilst working the 09.24 Victoria-Uckfield service. The signal was removed following closure of the Tunbridge Wells-Groombridge line. *John Vaughan*

*Below:*

In 1981 two prototype DEMUs, one 3-car and the other 4-car, emerged from Derby Works for evaluation and were classified as Class 210. Allocated to Reading depot and working regularly on the Paddington suburban services they have proved popular, but further construction is unlikely on the grounds of cost. On 1 November 1984 the 3-car unit No 210002 waits to depart from Paddington as the 15.04 to Reading. *Colin J. Marsden*

*Far right:*

By far the largest fleet of DMUs operating on BR metals are the Metropolitan-Cammell Class 101 sets with over 600 cars of the same basic design being constructed over a four year period from 1956. They can be coupled into 2-, 3- or 4-car formations and, here, a 2-car London Midland Region set passes Marsh Brook in the Border Counties, on the old 'North & West' Route, forming the 15.50 Shrewsbury-Swansea service. The train will take to the Central Wales line at Craven Arms. *John Vaughan*

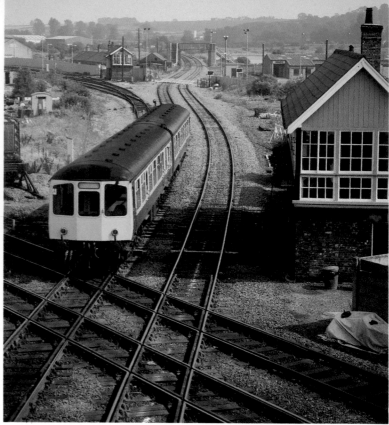

*Above left:*
**Passengers board BR Derby Class 108 driving trailer composite No M54269 at Manchester Victoria on 30 May 1984. This substantial fleet of low density units numbers over 300 and can be coupled into 2-, 3- or 4-car formations. All are allocated to Eastern and London Midland Regions.**
*Brian Morrison*

*Above:*
**On 21 August 1984, a 2-car Birmingham RC&W DMU of Class 110 departs eastwards from Lincoln Central and passes over Pelham Street Crossing, forming the 14.37 to Boston. These Rolls-Royce-engined 'Calder Valley' units date from 1961 and all are allocated to the Eastern Region.**
*Bill Sharman*

*Left:*
**Another of the larger DMU classes when constructed from 1956-59 was the Cravens Class 105, with nearly 250 cars in service. Drastic inroads into them have been made, however, and it will not be long before a scene such as this at Newcastle on 29 May 1980 will be something from the past. A 2-car Class 105 leads here with a local train for Alnmouth.** *Brian Morrison*

*Above right:*
**An interesting development of recent years is the prototype Class 140 DMU developed at Derby Works from the LEV railbus and constructed from Leyland National bus body components, mounted on a railway underframe. On 18 April 1985 the unit appeared unexpectedly with a Plymouth-Par driver training special and is seen passing Tywardreath near Par in Cornwall.** *John Vaughan*

*Right:*
**Another type of DMU which closely follows the standard design are the 15 3-car units that make up the Birmingham RC&W Class 118. Introduced in 1959 for Western Region suburban use, all are allocated to Plymouth Laira or Bristol Bath Road, On 17 April 1985 a unit reduced to a twin set passes Luxulyan forming the 17.43 Par-Newquay service, made up of DMS No W51320 and DMBS No W51305.**
*John Vaughan*

*Top right:*

Built for BR by Gloucester RC&W in 1958, the 25 Cross-country sets that make up Class 119 all have the familiar 'Derby' front end appearance. Due to line closures, members of the class have been quite extensively moved about the country and all have had their original buffets taken out of use. A present-day role for the Reading-based units is upon the Reading-Tonbridge and Reading-Gatwick Airport trains where the buffet area has been replaced by passenger luggage space. On an autumnal 15 November 1984, unit No L579 traverses Southern Region metals beneath the North Downs, near Dorking, and forms the 12.12 Gatwick Airport-Reading service.
*John Vaughan*

*Right:*

The Class 120 Cross-country 3-car DMUs were constructed at Swindon Works between 1957 and 1960. Like the Class 119s they have been switched about from area to area as a result of line closures, and the original buffet areas are now removed. On 27 June 1983, a 3-car unit running with a Metro-Cammell centre trailer forms a Matlock-Derby train approaching Duffield.
*Brian Morrison*

*Bottom right:*

The fleet of 15 single power cars and eight driving trailer seconds that makes up the 23 coaches of the Pressed Steel Co-built Class 121 were constructed in 1960 for branch line and local services and, in many ways, were the BR equivalent of the original GWR Railcars. For the GWR150 celebrations in 1985, certain locomotives and stock were painted in the GWR livery of chocolate and cream. One of the examples was Class 121 DMBS No W55020 which, on 20 July 1985, formed the 16.05 Ealing Broadway-Greenford local service.
*John Vaughan*

166

Above:
The Gloucester RC&W single parcels vans are known as DMLVs and are classified as Class 128. All are provided with a driving position at each end and three sets of double doors along the bodyside for mail and goods, and they have two Leyland Albion 6-cylinder engines of 230bhp. One such car, No W55991, scuttles down the Western main line near Twyford on 21 June 1984 forming the 15.55 Paddington-Reading parcels service. *Brian Morrison*

*Left:*
A derivative of the prototype Class 140 is the wide-bodied Leyland National/BR Derby Class 142 DMU which entered service on BR during late 1985. No 142008 passes Colleyhurst, Miles Platting, on 9 November 1985 smartly attired in the attractive livery of the Greater Manchester PTE.
*Hugh Ballantyne*

*Below left:*
Two Class 150 3-car prototype DMUs were constructed at BREL York Works in 1984, one powered by 285bhp Cummins engines and the second with 280bhp Rolls-Royce 'Eagles'. On 24 May 1985 the Rolls-Royce-powered unit No 150002 is pictured at Matlock after working the 14.20 train from Derby. *Stuart Marshall*

*Right:*
The Class 253 and 254 InterCity 125 trains were introduced from 1976 and 1977 respectively. The 253s consist of a rake of seven or eight Mk 3 coaches with a power car at each end, whilst the 254s include eight or nine cars to allow for the slightly higher loadings required on the East Coast main line services. With the changeover from the original blue and grey livery to the red and grey of the InterCity Sector, mixed formations with power cars and trailers in different combinations of colours were a common sight. On 11 January 1986, the 07.00 Plymouth-Newcastle train passes Church Road, south of Birmingham. *A. Swift*

*Below:*
Ordered at the same time as the prototype Class 150 units were the futuristic-looking Metropolitan-Cammell Class 151 prototypes which arrived at Derby in 1985 for evaluation. On 17 April 1985 two cars of 3-car unit No 151001 climb the Lickey Bank on test from Bromsgrove. *Brian J. Robbins*

*Above:*
The mammoth fleet of Class 08 diesel shunters once totalled 1,193 examples and many are still in service today — a tribute to the success of the design. Having been repainted in green at Tyseley, and carrying smart name and numberplates, No 08604 *Phantom* is seen at Birmingham New Street on 20 June 1986. *Chris Morrison*

*Below:*
The fleet of Class 20 Bo-Bo locomotives was introduced from 1957, built at the English Electric Vulcan Foundry. They are usually found coupled in pairs working on a variety of freight trains on Eastern, London Midland and Scottish Regions but are still used on passenger turns as the occasion demands. Also popular for railtours, Nos 20184 and 20169 are so employed rounding the sea wall approaching Teignmouth on 8 July 1984 with a special.
*Brian Morrison*

*Above:*

**The large fleet of Type 2 Bo-Bo Class 25 locomotives was introduced in 1961 as uprated versions of the Class 24s which entered service from 1957. They were constructed at the BR works of Crewe, Darlington and Derby and also at the Gorton Works of Beyer Peacock Ltd. Large numbers have been withdrawn during the past few years and their total demise is imminent. On 4 July 1985, Class 25/2 No 25200 passes Bayston Hill, in the delightful border country of Shrewsbury, with a load of ballast for Guide Bridge, the locomotive having run round its train at Dorrington.** *John Vaughan*

*Below:*

**Rather akin to the Class 24/25 relationship, the Class 27s are uprated and improved versions of the earlier Class 26s, which were the first main line diesel electric locomotives to be constructed at the Smethwick works of Birmingham RC&W from 1958, with the 1,250bhp Class 27 being introduced from 1960. Both types have spent most of their lives in Scotland. On 5 June 1982 No 27018 leaves Markinch with the 09.21 Edinburgh-Dundee service.** *B. Galloway*

*Above:*

The Class 31 A1A-A1A fleet of Type 2 locomotives was introduced during the days of steam in 1957 and constructed at the Loughborough Works of Brush Electrical Machines Ltd. Earlier teething troubles overcome, the locomotives are now a success story and can be seen on all four English Regions hauling a variety of both passenger and freight traffic. Passing Clay Cross Junction on 26 June 1985, No 31309 hauls a down freight off the Erewash Valley line. *Les Nixon*

*Right:*

To satisfy the Southern Region's requirements for a main line locomotive fleet in the Type 3 category, an order for 98 was given to the BRC&W Co for construction at their Smethwick Works and the first emerged in 1959. The same basic body shell as that used on the Class 26s was utilised with a number of detail differences. The power unit, however, was an excellent 1,550bhp Sulzer. This pair of 'Cromptons' was photographed at Basingstoke on 29 September 1984. On the left is Class 33/1 'push-pull' variant No 33111 with the 14.10 Waterloo-Salisbury, while on the right is Class 33/0 No 33012 with the diverted Cardiff Central-Portsmouth Harbour service. *John Vaughan*

*Below right:*

The 230 locomotives of Class 37 were constructed between 1960 and 1965 by both the English Electric Co at Newton-le-Willows and by the Robert Stephenson & Hawthorn Works at Darlington. Powered by an English Electric 12CSVT engine producing up to 1,750bhp these Type 3 Co-Co locomotives can literally be seen from Caithness to Cornwall, where they operate with equal success. No 37165 leaves Standedge Tunnel at Diggle on 26 March 1982 with a westbound haul of tanks. *Bill Chapman*

*Above:*
**Surely the most famous locomotive running on BR during the mid-1980s must be green-liveried Class 40 No 40122/D200, retained for use on special services such as this Scottish Railway Preservation Society charter to Kyle of Lochalsh, seen at Gleneagles on 28 June 1986.** *Bert Wynn*

*Right:*
**During 1985 a number of withdrawn Class 40 1Co-Co1 locomotives were resuscitated from the scrap lines for use as departmental locomotives during the big Crewe re-signalling operation. Standing at the head of an overhead catenary special working on 3 July 1985 is the former No 40118, renumbered 97408.**
*John Vaughan*

*Above:*
Passing through delightful countryside at Respryn Bridge, between Lostwithiel and Bodmin Parkway stations, on 18 April 1985 is 'Peak' Class 45/0 No 45069 hauling the 09.38 ABS freight from St Blazey to Severn Tunnel Junction. The original 10 Sulzer-engined 2,300bhp 'Peaks', designated Class 44, were withdrawn from service in 1980. The main batch of this Type 4 1Co-Co1 design, had an uprated 2,500bhp Sulzer engine and was divided into three types: the steam heat boilered 45/0s, those fitted for electric train heating and classified 45/1, and the batch fitted with Brush electrical equipment and given TOPS classification 46. Overall the 'Peaks' have given outstanding service to BR for over a quarter of a century.  *John Vaughan*

*Below:*
The Brush Group's Falcon Works at Loughborough produced the first of the Class 47s in September 1962. By early 1967, no fewer than 512 locomotives of the class had been built at Loughborough and at BR Crewe and the excellent Type 4 had become the largest class of main line diesel-electric locomotive in the country. In the last week of operation of Ely South signalbox, Class 47/4 No 47506 blasts away from Ely past the many semaphore signals that have now been removed, hauling the 17.30 for Liverpool Street on 20 June 1985.  *John Vaughan*

**Fifty Class 50s were built by English Electric at their Vulcan Foundry Works at Newton-le-Willows in 1967-68 for use on the northern sections of the West Coast main line that had still to be electrified. Fitted for multiple-unit working by Crewe Works in 1969, the 2,700bhp machines succesfully worked in pairs with heavy trains over the severely graded route, including Shap and Beattock Banks, until the fully electrified Euston-Glasgow service started in May 1975. Prior to this, some of the class had been undergoing trials on Western Region and, eventually, all were transferrred to Old Oak Common, Bristol and Laira, allowing the WR to withdraw the much-loved but non-standard Class 52 'Western' fleet. Advent of the HSTs resulted in the class being found work on the Waterloo-Exeter services and on many of the inter-regional expresses to and from the West Country. On 3 July 1984, No 50010** *Monarch* **forges through the Devon countryside at Worth, near Exeter, with the 10.27 Paddington-Penzance express which consists of all first class stock.** *Brian Morrison*

*Left:*

A significant increase in the movement of coal by rail required a Type 5 freight locomotive capable of heavy, long-distance haulage. The success of the Class 47s ensured that Brush obtained the contract for the first 30 machines, which were built at the Brush Group's Romanian counterpart of Electroputere which commenced delivery in 1976. BREL Doncaster took up the building from No 56031 and the total fleet of 135 locomotives was completed at Crewe to allow Doncaster to make a start on the Class 58s. On 16 June 1984 No 56031 *Merehead* is seen near the village of Great Bedwyn, on the Berks & Hants line, hauling Yeoman Procor stone hoppers towards Westbury.
*John Vaughan*

*Above:*

Constructed by General Motors of the USA, four Co-Co diesel-electric locomotives powered by GM 16-cylinder engines of the same 3,300bhp output as the Class 58s, were delivered to these shores in 1985 to the order of Foster Yeoman for exclusive use on their stone trains to and from Merehead Quarry, near Frome. Being allowed to operate over BR metals, they have been designated TOPS Class 59. Prior to being named *Yeoman Challenger*, No 59004 departs from Acton Yard with stone for Northfleet terminal.
*Jean Marsden*

*Below left:*

Despite the success of the Class 56s they were an expensive locomotive to construct. Present-day finances and technology brought about Class 58. This Type 5 locomotive is of a completely new design, being assembled from 'pre-made' component parts bolted on to a rigid frame. Power is provided by a 12-cylinder GEC-Ruston engine capable of 3,300bhp. Fifty of the type have been constructed at BREL Doncaster, with the first delivered in November 1982. On 19 June 1985, No 58015 works into Westhouses with empty HAA Merry-go-round hoppers. *John Vaughan*

*Below:*

The 09.48 Southampton-Halling 'Rugby Cement' train passes Farnborough on 6 August 1983 headed by Class 73/0 electro-diesel No 73003. Capable of operating from the Southern Region third rail or being able to obtain traction from their own diesel engine/generator set, the class of 49 locomotives was constructed from 1962 at Eastleigh Works and from 1965 at English Electric's Vulcan Foundry. The electro-diesel concept was a very clever one and it is perhaps surprising that the principle has not been furthered on other regions of BR. *R. T. Nunn*

*Top:*
**On 17 August 1984, Class 81 electric locomotive No 81019 prepares to depart from Euston with a summer special of Mk 1 stock whilst, in the background, Class 87/0 No 87032 *Kenilworth* awaits departure time with the 15.50 for Manchester Piccadilly. The Class 81s were the first of the West Coast main line's new fleet of locomotives, having been ordered from Associated Electrical Industries who, in turn, sub-contracted the actual locomotive construction to Birmingham RC&W; they were introduced for driver and staff training from November 1959. The Class 82s appeared in May 1960 from AEI/Metrovick with building undertaken by Beyer Peacock; the Class 83s came from English Electric; the Class 84s from the North British Locomotive Co of Glasgow; and the Class 85s from AEI/GEC with the construction taking place at BR Doncaster.** *Brian Morrison*

*Above:*
**Having gained considerable experience in the operation of electric locomotives, British Rail set about the introduction of a second generation of 100 machines, the Class 86s. Equipment for these was supplied by AEI/English Electric, mechanical construction being undertaken by BR Doncaster and English Electric. The Class 87s appeared in 1973 from BREL Crewe, with equipment supplied by GEC Traction Ltd, and with GEC traction motors generating 5,000bhp compared to the 3,600bhp from the AEI equipment in the Class 86s. The differing front end appearance of the two types is obvious from this scene at Euston with Class 86/2 No 86220 *Goliath* on the left and No 87012 *Coeur de Lion* on the right waiting to depart with expresses for Liverpool Lime Street and Carlisle.** *Brian Morrison*

# FIFTEEN

# BR LIVERIES FOR THE 1980s

There is no doubt that British Rail is rapidly losing its old 'corporate image' as local colour schemes take over both motive power and stock from one end of the system to the other. From Highland Rail and ScotRail, from the InterCity, Railfreight, Network SouthEast and Provincial Sectors and from the likes of the PTEs of Strathclyde, West Yorkshire, Greater Manchester and West Midlands comes a variety of colour that is supplemented by odd variants of GWR brown and cream, GWR lined green, British Telecom yellow, Red Star red and the strange looking maroon and white apparition sponsored by a local tourist authority with regard to a West

Highland shuttle! Some of the liveries are elegant, some are attractive but not very functional, and others are downright weird. More are yet to come no doubt as the fashion takes hold. At least it provides a field-day for the colour photographer.

*Below:*
**With power car No 43125 *Merchant Venturer* bringing up the rear of the train, the 07.45 Paddington-Penzance crosses Tregeagle Viaduct, between St Austell and Truro, on 24 August 1985 beautifully turned out in complete InterCity livery.** *John Vaughan*

*Top:*
**Highland Rail livery, with the large Scottish terrier emblem
relative to the size of the bodyside number and BR logo,
adorns the flanks of Class 37 No 37188** *Jimmy Shand*
**hauling a weed-killing train down the Oban line on 31 May
1985 and passing Tyndrum Lower.** *Dorothy Robinson*

*Above:*
**On 17 August 1985 new-look Scottish Class 26 No 26026 in
Railfreight livery brightens up the environs of Perth.**
*Tom Noble*

*Top right:*
**Class 37/4 No 37426** *Bont-y-Bermo* **heads the 10-coach
formation of InterCity-liveried Mk 1 stock making up the
07.25 summer Saturdays only Birmingham-Aberystwyth
train at Ynyslas on 9 August 1986.** *Geoffrey Bannister*

*Right:*
**In a breathtaking setting at Golant on the River Fowey,
Class 37 No 37196** *Tre Pol and Pen,* **in attractive Railfreight
livery, works in multiple with No 37222 heading down the
Fowey Branch with loaded china clay hoods on the
brilliantly clear evening of 3 October 1985.** *Brian Morrison*

*Above:*
**The first locomotive to appear in the Railfreight Sector's distinctive livery was Class 58 No 58001, seen here passing along the Crewe Independent Lines during the period that Crewe station was closed for major resignalling and relaying of trackwork. The train is a Garston-Toton coal empties and was photographed on 3 July 1985.**
*John Vaughan*

*Below:*
**The large fleet of Class 47s seems destined to appear in a variety of liveries, from the Stratford-applied silver roof and black window surrounds, through ScotRail, InterCity, GWR Green, Network SouthEast, Railfreight and large logo and number types to just plain blue. Sporting the colours of the Railfreight Sector, No 47050 hauls a train of tanks from Immingham to Sheffield Tinsley on 22 August 1985 and passes Mexborough.** *Michael J. Collins*

*Top:*
**Introduced in 1957 in, what was then, BR green with a silver roof and subsequently given the corporate treatment of 'Rail blue', few people may have expected the Class 20 fleet to appear in Railfreight grey but, in fact, they are being so treated — and very flattering it looks too on No 20023 seen at Tyseley, Birmingham, on 27 April 1985.** *T. R. Dungate*

*Above:*
**Another type to justify the new Railfreight image is the Class 31/1. On 5 September 1985 No 31158 approaches Shaldon Bridge, Teignmouth, hauling an up parcels train.**
*Stephen Montgomery*

The first Class 47 to receive InterCity paintwork was
No 47406 *Railriders* seen here near Durham on 4 November
1985 hauling the 09.23 Newcastle-Penzance train. It will be
pleasant when all the stock can match the locomotives.
*Peter J. Robinson*

*Below:*
InterCity Sector livery looks particularly smart when it is
kept clean and when the coaching stock matches. With a
Mk 3 sleeping car coupled next to the locomotive, Class 87/0
No 87016 *Sir Francis Drake* is pictured at Euston with the
17.03 service for Holyhead on 13 August 1986. *John E. Oxley*

*Bottom:*
When put into BR's plain blue livery the Class 73
electro-diesel fleet looked particularly mundane and rather
akin to the oft-described 'box on wheels'. Some now sport
the livery of the InterCity Sector for operating the 'Gatwick
Express' diagrams, whilst others, including the first
member of the class, No 73001, have received the attractive
grey roof, black window surrounds and large BR logo and
TOPS number treatment. On 30 May 1986, the Class 73/0
waits to depart Clapham yard with empty coaching stock.
*Brian Morrison*

*Below:*
**During the months of resignalling the Brighton main line, certain Inter-Regional trains started their journey from Hove, on the West Coastway line. On 7 May 1985 there was an interloper of note. Sporting its large Scottish terrier motif is No 47593 *Galloway Princess* waiting to leave the sidings at Hove with the 08.50 Hove-Manchester Piccadilly service. When would it again see its native Scotland?**
*John Vaughan*

*Bottom:*
**Inside 'B' Shop at Ilford in April 1986, ex-North British Class 84 electric locomotive No 84009 is in use solely for provision of the electricity required for the conversions taking place of TSO(T) coaches to 'Choice Express' Catering RMB(T)s for use on the then forthcoming cross-London InterCity services. The locomotive's paintwork and number, ADB968021, both reflect that it is now a departmental vehicle.** *Brian Morrison*

*Above:*
To celebrate the 150th anniversary of the Great Western Railway, four Class 47s were repainted into GWR lined green. They were Nos 47079 *G. J. Churchward*, 47484 *Isambard Kingdom Brunel*, 47500 *Great Western* and 47628 *Sir Daniel Gooch*. On 14 September 1985 No 47484 waits to leave Paddington with the 09.15 Paddington-Hereford 'Red Dragon' Chartex. *John Vaughan*

*Below:*
As the last of the sub-class to be given a full classified overhaul and repaint, the opportunity was taken to put Class 33/0 No 33008 *Eastleigh* back into the closest form of original green livery that regulations now allow. On a particularly drab 6 June 1986, the locomotive leads standard Rail blue No 33031 into Clapham Junction prior to propelling the 11.08 vans train from Eastleigh into Clapham Yard. *Brian Morrison*

*Left:*
On the evening prior to the Network SouthEast launch, the first Class 47 to be given their distinctive colours was displayed at Liverpool Street for its official naming of *The London Standard*. Following the ceremony, No 47573 is caught by the camera just prior to returning to Stratford Traction Repair Shop for the Network SouthEast lettering to be included on the bodysides for the official 'brand name' unveiling on the following morning. *Brian Morrison*

*Below:*
Class 50 'Hoover' No 50017 *Royal Oak* in Network SouthEast red, white, blue and grey heads the 15.10 Waterloo-Exeter St Davids train through Clapham cutting on 21 June 1986. *Chris Morrison*

*Top:*
**Although the majority of the London termini had a part to play in the Network SouthEast launch on 10 June 1986, it was at Waterloo that the main ceremony took place. To prelude events two trains were simultaneously driven into platforms 1 and 2, with Class 50 No 50023 *Howe* on the left and an 8-car 455/8 formation consisting of sets Nos 5850 and 5872 on the right. All the stock of both trains was painted in the new Sector colours.** *Brian Morrison*

*Above:*
**In special livery for the Oban-Crianlarich summer shuttle, a BRC&W Class 104 DMU No 104325, in maroon and white livery, waits to depart Oban on 10 May 1985.** *J. Reside*

*Top:*
**Eastern Region's 'Stourton Saloon' made up of an old
Gloucester RC&W Class 100 twin set, and now numbered
TDB975664/975637, is pictured at Cargo Fleet,
Middlesbrough, on 30 September 1985 running an officers'
special from the British Steel works at Lackenby to York.
The set was given this distinctive paint job at Ilford Depot
where, surprisingly, the small yellow warning panel was
included.** *Peter J. Robinson*

*Above:*
**A 'new generation' DMU with a new generation livery.
Dressed up in the distinctive Provincial Sector colours,
Class 150/1 set No 150106 runs down to the Spital Bridge
stabling point at Peterborough on 6 March 1986 whilst
engaged on crew training turns.** *Bill Sharman*

*Left:*
**The blue and canary yellow colours of the West Midlands PTE are carried by Class 312 EMU No 312204 on 28 September 1985 forming the 14.21 service from Birmingham New Street to Coventry. The unit is pulling away from Lea Hall station having made the required stop.** *Robert Jones*

*Below left:*
**Nicely turned out in GWR chocolate and cream in connection with the GWR150 celebrations, Pressed Steel Co 3-car DMU No B430 passes Ashton Junction on 27 May 1985 forming the 12.10 Bristol Temple Meads-Portishead special. DMS No W51410 leads.** *Stephen Montgomery*

*Below:*
**Stratford Traction Repair Shop (TRS) has long had a reputation for providing something special with its charges so far as embellishments are concerned. From making their own nameplates, to providing Union Jack bodysides for a royal wedding, to silver roofs, the staff excelled even themselves in April 1986 when they returned the oldest surviving DMU in BR service to its original green livery with front whiskers. Proudly on display outside the TRS on 11 April is the Cravens Class 105 consisting of driving trailer second (DTS) No E54122 and driving motor brake second (DMBS) No E53359. The unit went on to work the last days of a diesel service on the Southminster and Sudbury branches prior to EMUs taking over on 12 May.**
*Brian Morrison*

*Top:*
**Although rather work-stained, the distinctive colours of the West Yorkshire Passenger Transport Executive still stand out on this Class 141 2-car DMU set No 141018, comprising driving motor seconds Nos 55518 and 55538. The train is the 15.40 service from Marsden to Leeds and is photographed prior to leaving Marsden on 12 March 1986.** *Larry Goddard*

*Above:*
**A Class 303 3-car EMU set painted in the attractive red livery of Strathclyde PTE, forms an Airdrie-Helensburgh train on 29 May 1985 and passes Bowling Harbour.**
*Tom Noble*

*Above right:*
**Not even the old 1959 Gloucester RC&W Co Class 128 parcels vans are excused from new colours! On 4 May 1986 No M55994 poses at Tyseley dressed in 'Red Star' red, white and blue.** *Robert Jones*

*Right:*
**The original London & South East Sector colours of brown,
orange and beige were applied to a number of Southern
Region Class 411/5 4-CEP EMU sets and a few of the 'Clacton
Express' Class 309s of Eastern Region — and very elegant
the livery looked too. The colours are likely to be retained
for some time on the stock now used for the electrified
Hastings services. On 23 May 1986 a 12-CEP combination,
with unit No 1534 leading, speeds through Petts Wood
station forming an evening '1066 Route' train from Charing
Cross to Hastings.** *Brian Morrison*

# SIXTEEN

# MISCELLANY

## BRIDGES AND VIADUCTS

A 2-car Class 141 DMU forms the 09.40 Leeds-York train on 19 August 1984 and crosses the River Wharfe by way of the Arthington Viaduct, near Bramhope. *Bill Sharman*

*Above:*

The Western main line from Saltash to Penzance, in Cornwall, contains 32 substantial viaducts in its length of just over 75 miles, and the one at Coombe St Stephen, between Burngullow and Truro, is as impressive as any. On 3 October 1985, Class 50 'Hoover' No 50003 *Temeraire* crosses with the five coaches that make up the 11.20 Penzance-Plymouth service. *Brian Morrison*

*Below:*

The Kingsferry Bridge is the road and rail link from the Isle of Sheppey to the Kent mainland and is the third structure that has served the purpose since 1860. The present 270ton bridge dates from 1959; the central span is raised from the four 130ft towers, to allow craft to pass beneath, and the control room is linked to Sittingbourne signalbox as well as with the shipping traffic. On 6 September 1985, the Sittingbourne-Sheerness shuttle crosses formed of Class 411/5 4-CEP No 1563. *Brian Morrison*

# THE 'GATWICK EXPRESS'

*Right:*

**The main sphere of activity for the Class 73 electro-diesels prior to May 1984 was on a variety of freight diagrams and a few boat train workings. The decision to use them on the new 'Gatwick Express' service completely changed what had gone before and the new 15-minute interval service between London Victoria and Gatwick Airport resulted in Class 33s taking over a number of their previous duties. On the day that the services were inaugurated, No 73123, painted in InterCity livery to match the new stock, was named *Gatwick Express* and carried a special headboard to mark the occasion.** *Brian Morrison*

*Below:*

**The Class 73s, for the most part, haul the trains from Victoria and propel them from Gatwick. The stock is made up of a rake of rebuilt Mk 2 air-conditioned coaches with a Gatwick Luggage Van (GLV) rebuilt from redundant HAP motor coaches. With GLV No 9104 leading, and No 73113 bringing up the rear, an up 'Gatwick Express' passes a 4-BIG EMU heading a down Littlehampton/Portsmouth Harbour service between Clapham Junction and Wandsworth Common on the same day.** *Brian Morrison*

# PROBLEMS OF WINTER

*Top:*
**At Borwick, near Carnforth, on 12 December 1981, a four-car Class 108 DMU formation traverses a suitably seasonal landscape as the 11.24 train from Morecambe to Leeds on 12 December 1981.** *Bill Sharman*

*Above:*
**Class 423 4-VEP EMU No 7823 hurries away from Basingstoke forming the 09.12 Bournemouth-Waterloo service, also on 12 December 1981.**
*Les Bertram*

*Right:*
**Working in multiple, Class 37s Nos 37200 and 37070 power a rake of tanks on the Copy Pit line in the late winter of 1981.** *Graham Roose*

*Left:*
**The lamps on the buffer stops cast a rather strange red glow on to snowplough No ADM965228 and Class 104 trailer car No M59228 at Buxton on 21 February 1985.** *Brian Morrison*

*Above:*
**A pair of BRC&W Class 26/0s, Nos 26034 and 26041, await departure time at Aberdeen on the evening of 14 November 1984 with a train for Inverness.** *Colin J. Marsden*

*Below left:*
**On the cold night of 21 February 1985, the yard lights at Buxton illuminate Class 45/0 'Peak' No 45044 and Class 20 No 20135. Both locomotives are stabled for the night having brought in earlier freight workings.** *Brian Morrison*

*Below:*
**Just one week earlier, on 7 November 1984, the same photographer is at Doncaster to record Brush Class 31/4 No 31446 heading the 21.00 to Hull.** *Colin J. Marsden*

*Top:*
**A colourful and interesting scene at the BREL Works, Doncaster, with Class 58 No 58025 under construction on 20 November 1984.** *Colin J. Marsden*

*Above:*
**On 8 May 1984, Class 87/0 No 87007 *City of Manchester* receives attention inside Willesden Depot.** *Brian Morrison*

*Left:*
**Inside Stratford's Traction Repair Shop on 16 January 1986, two Class 37s and a variety of Class 47s receive attention for, inter alia, power unit repairs, derailment and collision damage, bogie overhaul, tyre turning and a fire alarm earth fault.** *Brian Morrison*

# THE TRAVELLING POST OFFICE

*Right:*
**Birmingham RC&W Class 26/0 Bo-Bo No 26033 hammers through the rock cutting at Nigg Bay, south of Aberdeen, on 29 March 1974 hauling the 15.30 Aberdeen-Perth Special TPO. The first of the four passenger carriages which are permitted to be conveyed with this train is just visible.**
*Brian Morrison*

*Below:*
**With the sun very low in the sky, the 19.22 Penzance-Paddington TPO leaves the Cornish terminus behind on the first day of May 1985 and is powered eastwards by Class 50 'Hoover' No 50005 *Collingwood*.** *Jean Marsden*

# APPENDICES

## Diesel Locomotives

| Class | Wheel type | Introduced | Built | Engine | Power |
|---|---|---|---|---|---|
| 03 | 0-6-0DM | 1958 | BR Swindon & Doncaster | Gardner 4-cyl | 204bhp |
| 08 | 0-6-0DE | 1953 | BR Darlington, Derby, Doncaster, Crewe & Horwich | EE 6-cyl | 350bhp |
| 08/9 | 0-6-0DE | Rebuilt from Class 08 | | EE 6-cyl | 350bhp |
| 09 | 0-6-0DE | 1959 | BR | EE 6-cyl | 350bhp |
| 20 | Bo-Bo | 1957 | English Electric | EE 8-cyl | 1,000bhp |
| 25/1 | Bo-Bo | 1963 | BR Darlington & Derby | Sulzer 6-cyl | 1,250bhp |
| 25/2 | Bo-Bo | 1963 | BR Darlington & Derby | Sulzer 6-cyl | 1,250bhp |
| 25/3 | Bo-Bo | 1966 | BR Derby/Beyer Peacock | Sulzer 6-cyl | 1,250bhp |
| 25/9 | Bo-Bo | Converted from Class 25/3 | | Sulzer 6-cyl | 1,250bhp |
| 26/0 | Bo-Bo | 1958 | Birmingham RC&W | Sulzer 6-cyl | 1,160bhp |
| 26/1 | Bo-Bo | 1959 | Birmingham RC&W | Sulzer 6-cyl | 1,160bhp |
| 27/0 | Bo-Bo | 1961 | Birmingham RC&W | Sulzer 6-cyl | 1,250bhp |
| 31/1 | A1A-A1A | 1959 | Brush Traction | EE 12-cyl | 1,470bhp |
| 31/4 | A1A-A1A | Converted from Class 31/0 | | EE 12-cyl | 1,470bhp |
| 33/0 | Bo-Bo | 1960 | Birmingham RC&W | Sulzer 8-cyl | 1,550bhp |
| 33/1 | Bo-Bo | 1960 | Birmingham RC&W | Sulzer 8-cyl | 1,550bhp |
| 33/2 | Bo-Bo | 1962 | Birmingham RC&W | Sulzer 8-cyl | 1,550bhp |
| 37/0 | Co-Co | 1960 | English Electric | EE 12-cyl | 1,750bhp |
| 37/4 | Co-Co | 1985 | See note | EE 12-cyl | 1,750bhp |
| 37/5 | Co-Co | 1986 | See note | EE 12-cyl | 1,750bhp |
| 37/7 | Co-Co | 1986 | See note | EE 12-cyl | 1,750bhp |
| 37/9 | Co-Co | 1986 | See note | Mirrlees/Ruston | 1,750bhp |
| 40 | 1Co-Co1 | 1958 | English Electric | EE 16-cyl | 2,000bhp |
| 45/0 | 1Co-Co1 | 1960 | BR Derby & Crewe | Sulzer 12-cyl | 2,500bhp |
| 45/1 | 1Co-Co1 | 1960 | BR Derby & Crewe | Sulzer 12-cyl | 2,500bhp |
| 47/0 | Co-Co | 1962 | Brush/BR Crewe | Sulzer 12-cyl | 2,580bhp |
| 47/3 | Co-Co | 1964 | Brush | Sulzer 12-cyl | 2,580bhp |
| 47/4 | Co-Co | 1962 | Brush/BR Crewe | Sulzer 12-cyl | 2,580bhp |
| 47/7 | Co-Co | 1979 | See note | Sulzer 12-cyl | 2,580bhp |
| 47/9 | Co-Co | 1979 | See note | Ruston 12-cyl | 3,250bhp |
| 50 | Co-Co | 1967 | English Electric | EE 16-cyl | 2,700bhp |
| 56 | Co-Co | 1977 | Electroputere/BREL Doncaster & Crewe | Ruston 16-cyl | 3,250bhp |
| 58 | Co-Co | 1983 | BREL Doncaster | Ruston 12-cyl | 3,300bhp |
| 59 | Co-Co | 1985 | General Motors | GM 16-cyl | 3,300bhp |

**Notes:**

37/4: Rebuilt from Class 37/0
37/5: Rebuilt from Class 37/0
37/7: Rebuilt from Class 37/0

37/9: Rebuilt from Class 37/0
47/7: Rebuilt from Class 47/4
47/9: Rebuilt from Class 47/0

# Electric Locomotives

| Class | Wheel type | Introduced | Built | Equipment | Power |
|---|---|---|---|---|---|
| 81 | Bo-Bo | 1960 | Birmingham RC&W | AEI | 3,200bhp |
| 82 | Bo-Bo | 1960 | Beyer Peacock | AEI | 3,300bhp |
| 83 | Bo-Bo | 1960 | English Electric | EE | 2,950bhp |
| 85 | Bo-Bo | 1961 | BR Doncaster | AEI | 3,200bhp |
| 86/1 | Bo-Bo | Rebuilt from Class 86/0 | | EE/AEI | 5,000bhp |
| 86/2 | Bo-Bo | Rebuilt from Class 86/0 | | EE | 4,040bhp |
| 86/4 | Bo-Bo | Rebuilt from Classes 86/0, 86/3 | | EE | 4,040bhp |
| 87/0 | Bo-Bo | 1973 | BREL Crewe | GEC | 5,000bhp |
| 87/1 | Bo-Bo | 1974 | BREL Crewe | GEC | 4,850bhp |
| 89 | Co-Co | 1980 | BREL Crewe | Brush | 5,830bhp |

**Note:**
Class 86/0: Introduced 1965, built BR Doncaster/English Electric

# Electro-diesel Locomotives

| Class | Wheel type | Introduced | Built | Engine | Power |
|---|---|---|---|---|---|
| 73/0 | Bo-Bo | 1962 | BR Eastleigh | EE 4-cyl | 600bhp diesel/ 1,600bhp electric |
| 73/1 | Bo-Bo | 1965 | English Electric | EE 4-cyl | 600bhp diesel/ 1,600bhp electric |

# InterCity 125 Power Cars

| Class | Wheel type | Introduced | Built | Engine | Power |
|---|---|---|---|---|---|
| 43 | Bo-Bo | 1976 | BREL Crewe | Paxman 12-cyl/Mirrlees | 2,250bhp |

# Diesel Multiple-Units

| Class | Type | Introduced | Built | Engines | Vehicles in unit |
|---|---|---|---|---|---|
| 100 | Low density | 1957 | Gloucester RC&W | AEC | See note |
| 101 | Low density | 1956 | Metro-Cammell | Leyland | 2/3 |
| 104 | Low density | 1957 | Birmingham RC&W | Leyland | 2/3 |
| 105 | Low density | 1956 | Cravens | Leyland | 2 |
| 107 | Low density | 1960 | BR Derby | Leyland | 3 |
| 108 | Low density | 1958 | BR Derby | Leyland | 2/3/4 |
| 110 | Low density | 1961 | Birmingham RC&W | Rolls-Royce | 2/3 |
| 111 | Low density | 1957 | Metro-Cammell | Rolls-Royce | 2/3 |
| 114 | Low density | 1956 | BR Derby | Leyland | 2 |
| 115 | High density | 1960 | BR Derby | Leyland | 4 |
| 116 | High density | 1957 | BR Derby | Leyland | 3 |
| 117 | High density | 1959 | Pressed Steel | Leyland | 3 |
| 118 | High density | 1960 | Birmingham RC&W | Leyland | 2/3 |
| 119 | Cross-country | 1958 | Gloucester RC&W | Leyland | 3 |
| 120 | Cross-country | 1957 | BR Swindon | AEC | 2/3 |
| 121 | High density | 1960 | Pressed Steel | Leyland | 1/2 |
| 122 | High density | 1958 | Gloucester RC&W | AEC | 1 |
| 127 | High density | 1959 | BR Derby | Non-powered | See note |
| 127 | Parcels | Rebuilt from Class 127 | | Rolls-Royce | 2 |
| 128 | Parcels | 1959 | Gloucester RC&W | Leyland | 1 |
| 141 | Local | 1983 | Leyland/BREL Derby | Leyland | 2 |
| 142 | Local | 1985 | Leyland/BREL Derby | Leyland | 2 |
| 143 | Local | 1985 | W. Alexander/A. Barclay | Leyland | 2 |
| 144 | Local | 1986 | W. Alexander/BREL Derby | Leyland | 2 |
| 150 | Provincial | 1984 | BREL York | Cummins/Rolls-Royce | 2/3 |
| 150/1 | Provincial | 1985 | BREL York | Cummins | 2 |
| 150/2 | Provincial | 1986 | BREL York | Cummins | 2 |
| 151 | Provincial | 1985 | Metro-Cammell | Cummins | 3 |
| 154 | Provincial | Rebuilt from Class 150 | | Cummins | 2/3 |
| 155 | Provincial | 1987 | Leyland | Cummins | 2 |
| 156 | Provincial | 1987 | Metro-Cammell | Cummins | 2 |

**Notes:**
Class 100: One vehicle only remains, formed as two-car unit with Class 105 car
Class 127. Trailer second vehicles only remain, formed within Class 116 units
Certain Class 101, 105, 116 & 120 power cars converted to operate as two-car parcels units

# Diesel-Electric Multiple-Units

| Class | Type | Introduced | Built | Engines | Vehicles in unit |
|---|---|---|---|---|---|
| 202, 203 | Main line | 1957 | BR Eastleigh | English Electric | 6/4 |
| 204 | Secondary | Rebuilt from Classes 205 & 206 | | English Electric | 3 |
| 205 | Secondary | 1957 | BR Eastleigh | English Electric | 3 |
| 205/1 | Secondary | Modified 1979 from Class 205 | | English Electric | 3 |
| 206/1 | Secondary | Modified 1986 from Class 205 | | English Electric | 3 |
| 207 | Secondary | 1962 | BR Eastleigh | English Electric | 3 |
| 210 | Outer-suburban | 1981 | BR Derby | Paxman/MTU | 3/4 |

*Left:*
**With the massive superstructure of the Forth Bridge in the background, Class 254 power car No 43101** *Edinburgh International Festival* **leads the 10.00 Aberdeen-King's Cross 'Aberdonian' express through Dalmeny on a sunny October day in 1984.** *John Vaughan*

# Electric Multiple-Units: Overhead Supply

| Class | Type | Introduced | Built | Equipment | Power supply | Vehicles in unit |
|---|---|---|---|---|---|---|
| 302 | Suburban | 1959 | BR Doncaster & York | EE | 6.25kV & 25kV ac | 4 |
| 303 | Suburban | 1959 | Pressed Steel | EE | 25kV ac | 3 |
| 304 | Suburban | 1960 | BR Wolverton | AEI | 25kV ac | 4 |
| 305/1 | Outer-suburban | 1960 | BR York | EE | 6.25kV & 25kV ac | 3 |
| 305/2 | Outer-suburban | 1960 | BR Doncaster | EE | 6.25kV & 25kV ac | 4 |
| 307 | Outer-suburban | 1956 | BR Eastleigh | EE | 6.25kV & 25kV ac | 4 |
| 308/1 | Suburban | 1961 | BR York | EE | 6.25kV & 25kV ac | 4 |
| 308/2 | Suburban | 1961 | BR York | EE | 6.25kV & 25kV ac | 3 |
| 308/3 | Suburban | 1901 | BR York | EE | 6.25kV & 25kV ac | 3 |
| 309/1 | Express | 1962 | BR York | EE | 6.25kV & 25kV ac | 4 |
| 309/3 | Express | 1962 | BR York | EE | 6.25kV & 25kV ac | 4 |
| 309/4 | Express | 1962 | BR York | EE | 6.25kV & 25kV ac | 4 |
| 310 | Semi-fast | 1965 | BR Derby | EE | 25kV ac | 4 |
| 311 | Suburban | 1967 | Cravens | AEI | 25kV ac | 3 |
| 312/0 | Semi-fast | 1977 | BREL York | GEC | 25kV ac | 4 |
| 312/1 | Semi-fast | 1975 | BREL York | GEC | 25kV ac | 4 |
| 312/2 | Semi-fast | 1976 | BREL York | GEC | 25kV ac | 4 |
| 313 | Suburban | 1976 | BREL York | GEC | 25kV ac & 750V dc | 3 |
| 314 | Suburban | 1979 | BREL York | GEC/Brush | 25kV ac | 3 |
| 315 | Suburban | 1980 | BREL York | GEC | 25kV ac | 4 |
| 317 | Outer-suburban | 1981 | BREL Derby & York | GEC | 25kV ac | 3 |
| 317/2 | Outer-suburban | 1985 | BREL Derby & York | GEC | 25kV ac | 3 |
| 318 | Outer-suburban | 1986 | BREL Derby & York | GEC | 25kV ac | 4 |
| 319 | Cross-London | | BREL York | | 25kV ac & 750V dc | 4 |

**Note:**
Class 319 to be introduced 1987

*Below:*
**In Network SouthEast livery, a BR Derby Class 310 EMU, looking very sprightly despite its 25 years, works a special train from Euston on 10 June 1986.** *Brian Morrison*

# Electric Multiple-Units: Third Rail

| Class | Type | Introduced | Built | Equipment | Power supply | Vehicles in unit |
|---|---|---|---|---|---|---|
| 411/3 (4-CEP) | Express | 1958 | BR Eastleigh | EE | 750V dc | 4 |
| 411/4 (4-CEP) | Express | 1956 | BR Eastleigh | EE | 750V dc | 4 |
| 411/5 (4-CEP) | Express | 1958 | BR Eastleigh | EE | 750V dc | 4 |
| 412/3 (4-BEP) | Express | 1956 | BR Eastleigh | EE | 750V dc | 4 |
| 413/2 (4-CAP) | Secondary | 1957 | BR Eastleigh | EE | 750V dc | 4 |
| 413/3 (4-CAP) | Secondary | 1958 | BR Eastleigh | EE | 750V dc | 4 |
| 414/2 (2-HAP) | Secondary | 1957 | BR Eastleigh | EE | 750V dc | 2 |
| 414/3 (2-HAP) | Secondary | 1958 | BR Eastleigh | EE | 750V dc | 2 |
| 415/1 (4-EPB) | Suburban | 1951 | BR Eastleigh | EE | 750V dc | 4 |
| 415/3 (4-EPB) | Suburban | 1960 | BR Eastleigh | EE | 750V dc | 4 |
| 415/4 (4-EPB) | Suburban | 1951 | BR Eastleigh | EE | 750V dc | 4 |
| 415/6 (4-EPB) | Suburban | 1960 | BR Eastleigh | EE | 750V dc | 4 |
| 416/2 (2-EPB) | Suburban | 1953 | BR Eastleigh | EE | 750V dc | 2 |
| 416/3 (2-EPB) | Suburban | 1953 | BR Eastleigh | EE | 750V dc | 2 |
| 416/4 (2-EPB) | Suburban | 1953 | BR Eastleigh | EE | 750V dc | 2 |
| 419 (MLV) | Luggage van | 1959 | BR Eastleigh | EE | 750V dc | 1 |
| 421/1 (4-CIG) | Express | 1964 | BR York | EE | 750V dc | 4 |
| 421/2 (4-CIG) | Express | 1970 | BREL York | EE | 750V dc | 4 |
| 421/3 (4-CIG) | Express | 1964 | BR York | EE | 750V dc | 4 |
| 421/4 (4-CIG) | Express | 1970 | BREL York | EE | 750V dc | 4 |
| 422/1 (4-BIG) | Express | 1965 | BR York | EE | 750V dc | 4 |
| 422/2 (4-BIG) | Express | 1970 | BREL York | EE | 750V dc | 4 |
| 423 (4-VEP) | Express | 1967 | BR/BREL York | EE | 750V dc | 4 |
| 432 (4-REP) | Express | 1967 | BR/BREL York | EE | 750V dc | 4 |
| 438 (4-TC) | Express trailer | 1966 | BR/BREL York | | | 4 |
| 455/7 | Suburban | 1984 | BREL York | GEC/Brush | 750V dc | 4 |
| 455/8 | Suburban | 1982 | BREL York | GEC | 750V dc | 4 |
| 455/9 | Suburban | 1985 | BREL York | GEC | 750V dc | 4 |
| 485 (5-VEC) | Isle of Wight | 1967 | Metro-Cammell/ Union Car Co/ Cammell Laird | BTH | 630V dc | 5 |
| 486 (2-TIS) | Isle of Wight | 1967 | Metro-Cammell/ Union Car Co/ Cammell Laird | BTH | 630V dc | 2 |
| 487 | Waterloo & City | 1940 | English Electric | EE | 600V dc | 2/5 |
| 488/2 | 'Gatwick Express' | 1983 | BREL Derby | | | 2 |
| 488/3 | 'Gatwick Express' | 1983 | BREL Derby | | | 3 |
| 489 | Driving luggage van | 1983 | BREL Eastleigh | EE | 750V dc | 1 |
| 504 | Suburban | 1959 | BR Wolverton | EE | 1,200V dc | 2 |
| 507 | Suburban | 1978 | BREL York | GEC | 750V dc | 3 |
| 508 | Suburban | 1979 | BREL York | GEC | 750V dc | 3 |

**Notes:**

411/3 & 411/5: Converted from Class 411/2, refurbished, 1975 & 1979
411/4: Converted from Class 411/1, refurbished, 1980
412/3: Converted from Class 410, refurbished, 1982
413/2 & 413/3: Formed of two former Class 414 two-car units (built 1956), 1982
415/4: Converted from Class 415/1, refurbished, 1978
415/6: Converted from Class 415/3, refurbished, 1983
416/3: Converted from Class 416/1, refurbished, 1983
416/4: Converted from Class 416/2, refurbished, 1985
421/3: Converted from Class 421/1 and Class 420/1, refurbished, 1985
421/4: Converted from Class 421/2, refurbished, 1986
422/1: Converted from Class 420/1, refurbished, 1985
422/2: Converted from Class 420/2, refurbished, 1985
438: Formerly Class 491
455/7: Includes former Class 508 trailer second
485 & 486: Converted from former London Transport underground stock, built 1923-1935
488/2 & 488/3: Converted from standard Mk 2f stock
489: Rebuilt from Class 414 motor brake second for 'Gatwick Express' service

The tables on pages 91-95 detail the BR fleet as at December 1986.

The much-loved 'Deltics' were the most powerful passenger diesel locomotives on BR, at 3,300bhp, and for almost 20 years dominated East Coast main line passenger services. No 55013 *The Black Watch* powers up Beattock Bank with a diverted King's Cross-Edinburgh train on 4 May 1980. *D. Rogers*

# SEVENTEEN

# BRITISH RAILWAYS
# THE FIRST
# TWENTY-ONE YEARS

# BRITISH RAILWAYS

## THE FIRST 21 YEARS

# 1947

The Transport Act 1947 receives its Royal Assent on 6th August.

The Big Four (SR,GWR,LNER and LMS) plus about fifty smaller concerns are replaced by a Commission (British Transport Commission), an Executive (The Railways Executive ), and six regions. The Act contains 170 pages, with 128 sections and 15 schedules.

Many of the clauses were never fully discussed, as the Government applied the guillotine to restrict the length of Committee hearings to debate the details of the Transport Bill 1946.

The name "British Railways" and its individual regions has no legal status as such, the legally-constituted body being in fact the British Transport Commission.

The BTC's function is to provide "an efficient, adequate, economical and properly integrated system of public inland transport and port facilities within Great Britain".

Shareholders of the private railways to be nationalised will be compensated with British Transport Stock, a Security guaranteed by the Government.

Half a million privately-owned railway wagons are to be compulsorily acquired.

LMS locomotive no.10000, built by English Electric

and Derby Works,is as yet the only main-line Diesel loco in service in the British Isles.

The snows of February/March 1947 are an especially testing time for the private railways in their last year of independence.

Safety is not at its best on a railway system still grievously run-down after the War Years, and there are many accidents:

21st January - South Bermondsey - in fog, empty steam train rams into rear of London Bridge to Crystal Palace electric train.

9th August - Doncaster - signalman forgets about first train, and clears signals for second train to run into it (both Kings Cross to Leeds services). Of 700 or so passengers in each train, 21 are killed and 188 injured in the tangled wreckage of the rear of the three coaches of the front train.

26th October - Goswick - Class A3 no.60066 *Merry Hampton*, diverting to the slow line, enters the crossover too fast, and is derailed, possibly due to an unauthorised friend on the the footplate distracting the driver's attention.

26th November - Farnborough - a rear-end collision as SR no.453 *King Arthur* runs into the train hauled by SR no.860 *Lord Hawke*.The three rear coaches are impacted, and two passengers are killed, because of the signalman not ensuring "line clear" after a power failure on the Automatic signals.

# 1948

At midnight on New Year's Eve 1947/8 steam locomotives sound their whistles to mark the new era of Nationalised railways. New Year's Day is not yet a Public Holiday, so it will be business as usual, and in fact little outward change will be visible on the railway for some time.

Sir Cyril Hurcomb, previously a civil servant, becomes chairman of BTC, the small policy-making organisation for PublicTransport undertakings. Sir Eustace Missenden, formerly of the Southern Railway, becomes chairman of the Railway Executive, the body entrusted with the actual running of the railways.

Six new Regions come into operation, with their own colours for station signs etc., to reinforce their identities:

| Region | Route Miles | Regional Colour |
|---|---|---|
| London Midland | 4,993 | Red |
| Western | 3,782 | Brown |
| Scottish | 3,730 | Light Blue |
| Eastern | 2,836 | Dark Blue |
| Southern | 2,250 | Green |
| North Eastern | 1,823 | Tangerine |

Upon Nationalisation, BR has taken over:

641,000 staff (85,000 of these employed in Workshops)
20,023 steam locos (of 448 types)
1,223,634 wagons (including 544,000 Private Owner wagons of 480 types)
56,000 coaching vehicles (2,609 less than 1939)
19,639 route miles (which will only fall to 19,222 during the subsequent six years of the Railway Executive)
52,254 miles of track

8,294 stations
973 marshalling yards

The normal life expectation of rolling stock and motive power is 35 years - in 1948, 39.3% of locos, 27.8% of wagons, and 23.6% of carriages exceed this criterion.

Non-steam locos inherited from the Big Four number only:
53 Diesel-Electric (mostly LMS shunters but including two 1600 h.p. English Electric main-line prototypes - there are also 40 railcars)
16 Electric (also 2,006 Electric motor vehicles)

Nationalisation also means the take-over of the private companies' ancillary interests:
Workshops for manufacture and repair of rolling stock
Road Vehicles
Hotels
Refreshment Rooms and train catering
Shipping services
Ports and harbours
Canals
as well as investments in:
Bus companies
Road haulage
Travel Agencies
Airlines
Pullman Car Co.Ltd.
Property Development
Commercial advertising sites

However, out of these, Buses are taken over by the Road Passenger Executive, and Lorries by the Road Haulage Executive, both organisations equivalent to the Railway Executive, in being under the policy-making umbrella of the BTC.

In March, a report "The Physical Condition of British Railways, January 1948" is published. It highlights arrears of maintenance, and abnormal wear and tear amounting to £179 million. However, passenger traffic is up 30% over pre-war levels, and freight 20% up.

The 1948 Summer timetable shows a train mileage overall 248,000 miles greater than in 1947. Total passenger journeys for the year will be 996,050,000.

New Construction in 1948:
> 299 Steam locos built in BR workshops
> 96 steam locos purchased from outside contractors
> 14 Diesel shunters
> 1 Electric loco
> (also: 558 secondhand War Department freight locos purchased from the Ministry of Supply)
> 1,334 coaches
> 39,167 wagons

In June, the first list of 12 Standard types of steam loco is drawn up. This will be the basis of the 1951-60 Standard loco-building programme, which will eventually number 999 locos.

In the pipeline, ordered by the Big Four, and still awaiting delivery, are:
> Two 1600 h.p. main-line Diesels for SR
> One 1600 h.p. Diesel-Mechanical "Fell" loco for LMR
> Two Gas-Turbine main-line locos for WR
> One 827 h.p. Diesel-Electric loco for secondary services on LMR

A surplus of 115,420 coal wagons (mostly grease-box-lubricated, rather than conventional modern oil-box types, and mostly over 37 years old) contrasts with a deficiency of 30,470 open goods wagons.

A report titled "Major Development Schemes: Five years 1948 to 1952" proposes £48 million to be spent on the infrastructure of BR.

In January, BR holds a "beauty contest" at Olympia for new loco liveries - represented are GWR Green, LNER Green, SR Malachite Green, and LNWR Black. In the Summer, 14 trains are painted in experimental liveries.
The schemes finally adopted are:

| Colour | Purpose | Lining |
|---|---|---|
| Blue (soon to be replaced by Brunswick Green) | The most powerful locos (8P) | Black/White |
| Brunswick Green | Express Passenger locos (5P-7P) | Orange/Black/Orange |
| Black | Mixed Traffic locos (0P-4P) | Red/Cream/Grey |
| Black | Freight locos | Unlined |
| "Plum & Spilt Milk" | Main-line corridor coaches | Yellow/Maroon/Yellow |
| Chocolate & Cream | Main-line corridor coaches | Black/Golden Yellow |
| Maroon | Local/Suburban coaches | Black/Golden Yellow |
| Green | Multiple-unit Electric trains | |

(lining later to be dropped for non-corridor and non-coaching stock)

From mid-April to September a series of Locomotive Exchanges take place, to evaluate the performances of locos outside their normal regions.Nothing much conclusive comes of the experiment, and all the locos revert to their normal stamping grounds. The categories of loco involved are Express Passenger, General Purpose, and Freight.

However, the Locomotive Testing Station at Rugby is opened on 19th October, and arguably represents a more scientific method of evaluating and comparing BR's collection of locos designed for the Big Four rivals, as well as future Standard construction.

The pre-war tradition of naming important trains is revived,with new additions as well as old favourites restored, e.g.:

> Royal Scot (Euston-Glasgow) restored
> Queen of Scots Pullman (Euston-Glasgow) restored
> Flying Scotsman (non-stop Kings Cross-Edinburgh) (new)
> Tees-Tyne Pullman (including the "Hadrian Bar") (new)
> South Yorkshireman (Marylebone-Bradford) (new)
> Thanet Belle (London-Ramsgate Pullman - later to be re-named Kentish Belle)
> Bournemouth Belle
> Brighton Belle
> Devon Belle
> Golden Arrow

During 12th and 13th August, all LNER lines between England and Scotland are cut, as a result of freak flood conditions, and seven bridges are down, or washed away.

In November, the BTC acquires the Thomas Tilling bus group, initially to be run by the Railway Executive.

The net traffic receipts for 1948 show an increase of £22.4m.

Railway Hotels and train catering are transferred from the Railways Executive to the Hotels Executive on 7th June, an administrative decision reflecting the uneasy relationship that will persist between railway operating and the ancillary aspects of rail travel.

BR's first year has a bad accident record:

17th April - Winsford - a Glasgow-Euston train is stopped, following the communication cord being pulled, and the following train is run into by another train, resulting in sixteen deaths in the last two coaches. A signalman had cleared the road for the next train, assuming that the first one had passed his box.

18th May - Wath Road - a St.Pancras to Bradford train is derailed on an embankment at 60-65 mph. Seven are killed, and the cause of the crash is put down to the rails having expanded in the hot weather.

18th May again - Ardler Junction - a converging collision, where the branch-line train driver misreads the signals, and proceeds in error. Three BR staff die, but no passengers.

17th July - New Southgate - Class A2 no.60508 *Duke of Rothesay*, hauling an Edinburgh to Kings Cross express, suffers derailment of its leading bogie in Barnet tunnel. The bogie then strikes the crossover south of the tunnel, destroying the track and derailing the whole train. The locomotive then falls over onto its right hand side, sliding a further 100 yards.The driver, whose train had earlier been exceeding the 60 mph speed limit by about 10 mph, escapes unharmed, but his fireman is killed as a result of being hit by wreckage from his own train following on behind.

30th November - Stockport - Due to a verbal misunderstanding, two trains (both Manchester-Buxton) that have been combined into one, start up and run into the rear of a stationary Manchester-Crewe train, telescoping two coaches. Five are Killed, and five are seriously wounded.

# 1949

Traffic has dropped since 1947, but on the credit side not a single passenger is killed in a train accident in 1949, the best record on the railways since 1908.

O.V.Bulleid, A.H.Peppercorn and F.W.Hawksworth, previously Chief Mechanical Engineers of the SR, LNER and GWR respectively, retire from BR service.

New named Express trains number 38 in all, including:

> Capitals Limited (London-Edinburgh non-stop)
> Bon Accord  (Glasgow-Aberdeen)
> St.Mungo  (Glasgow-Aberdeen)
> The Granite City  (Glasgow-Aberdeen)
> Fife Coast Express (Glasgow-St.Andrews)
> Irishman (Glasgow-Stranraer)
> Fenman (Liverpool St.-Hunstanton)

Main-line corridor coaches are now to be painted Crimson Lake with Cream upper panels (also known as Raspberry and Cream, or Blood and Custard), replacing the earlier Plum and Spilt Milk experimental livery.

357 new steam locos are constructed, all of pre-Nationalisation "Company" designs, as well as 32,000 wagons.

The last GWR "Bulldog" class loco, no.3341, is withdrawn - the last GW loco with a combined name and number plate.

The Liverpool Street-Shenfield Electrification is completed, and by the end of the year the service shows a 58% increase in usage over the corresponding period in 1948 - a dramatic example of the "Sparks Effect", whereby Electrification stimulates passenger take-up of services.

The Southern Region launches its double-decker electric train for use on the intensively-worked and overcrowded North Kent commuter services. It is not an overwhelming success, as loading time is increased, and the upper compartments are very subject to extremes of temperature.

The ER tracks from Loughton to Epping are electrified for the transfer of the line from BR to London Transport, as part of the extension to the Central Line.

Some statistics for 1949:
> Surplus on railway working: £12.7m.
> Net traffic receipts increased by £9m.
> Staff: 625,000
> Route miles at end of year: 19,573
> Meals served on restaurant cars: 11,800,000
> (generally the equivalent of 25p for breakfast and 30p for lunch or dinner)

New ships in BR ownership:
> MV *Hibernia*
> MV *Cambria*
> SS *Maid of Orleans*

In March, the Railway Executive's Commercial Advertising interests are taken away by the BTC. Also, a Central Traffic Costing Service and a Charges Division are created by the BTC, with a view to working towards an "integrated transport" scheme for all the Executives under its control.

In May, the NUR unsuccessfully claim a 10s.(50p) per week rise, plus extra pay for working Saturday afternoons and evenings.

In June, BR's investment in road haulage (e.g. Carter Patterson and Pickfords) is handed over to the new Road Transport Executive (which will later become the Road Haulage Executive, when split off from the Road Passenger Executive).

# 1950

The British Railways Rule Book 1950 is adopted for observance by the employees of the Railway Executive from 1st January 1950, and "all former rules which are inconsistent therewith or are made obsolete thereby shall be cancelled as from that date". Each employee supplied with this book "must make himself acquainted with, and will be held responsible for the observance of the following rules". It runs to 274 pages.

In January, a common Legal Service for all the Executives under the BTC is set up. The Railway Executive and London Transport have argued extensively to be considered as a separate case, but eventually accept the new structuring.

The blue livery for the largest express passenger locos is abandoned in favour of the Brunswick Green already applied to other locos in the higher power-ranges.

Stations and other installations are being given new signs, on backgrounds of their own regional colour. Names of stations are for the first time printed on the infamous enamel "double sausage" shaped signs.

Locos are now receiving the "Lion and Wheel" totem on their sides, replacing the earlier "British Railways" painstakingly written in full.

Steam loco construction for the year is 385, all "Company" designs, and 28,000 new wagons are built.

BR staff number 605,000, and at the end of the year route mileage stands at 19,471.

The first designs for the BR Mark 1 carriages are completed.

A mechanised foundry at Horwich, originally planned under the aegis of the LMS, comes into production.

9200 coal wagons are purchased from SNCF. Despite having been built for French railways in 1944-5 following the Liberation, little in the way of alteration is required, as they have been built to British standards. They are surplus to SNCF requirements.

The "Red Dragon" is the first named train for Paddington-South Wales services.

Various non-steam locos make their debut:
  1) A main-line Diesel-Electric of 1,750 h.p., with a wheel configuration of 1-Co-Co-1, originally ordered by the SR, built by English Electric and BR's Ashford Works, and numbered 10201.
  2) A mixed-traffic Diesel-Electric of 827 h.p., originally ordered by the LMS - a B-B with a Paxman power unit, built by BTH and North British, no.10800.
  3) A Gas-Turbine , ordered by the GWR, and built by Brown Boveri of Switzerland.

In April, the Regions are re-organised on a purely geographical, rather than "Line" basis, thereby divorcing the regional structure of BR even more from that of the old Companies. This effectively continues the policy of rationalisation of routes, begun earlier under Nationalisation.

In September, Southampton Docks are handed over from the Railway Executive to the Docks and Inland Waterways Executive.

In November, Swindon Works turns out the last 4-6-0 of purely GW design, in the form of "Modified Hall" Class no.7929 *Wyke Hall*.

The railway trades unions show their muscle during 1950, firstly with a demand from the NUR for a minimum £5 wage for all railwaymen, which is rejected. By August, the NUR is demanding an overall 10% wage increase, ASLEF is going after 15%, and the RCA (Railway Clerks Association - later to become the TSSA) puts in for 7.5%. A Ministry of Labour Court of Inquiry eventually settles the matter with an award of about 7.5%.

Net traffic receipts for the year show an increase of £23.5m, and the surplus on railway working is increased by £26.3m.

Meanwhile, connecting the railway systems of the UK with those of Europe are new rail ferry vessels, the SS *Amsterdam* for the Harwich-Hook service, and the SS *Brighton* for Newhaven-Dieppe.

Two accidents:

5th June - Tollerton - rails buckled by the sun derail Class A1 no.60153 *Flamboyant* and its train.

27th August - Penmaenmawr - a failure to follow rules leads to the up Irish Mail colliding at 60-70 mph with a light engine shunting in the station, and 5 passengers and 1 BR employee are killed.

Most ominously for BR's passenger revenue, 1950 is the year when petrol finally comes off the ration, leading to a rise in private car ownership.............

# 1951

The Festival of Britain includes various railway exhibits as part of the "New Elizabethan Era", including "Britannia" class locos nos.70004 *William Shakespeare* and 70014 *Iron Duke*, as well as electric loco class EM1 no.26020, perpetuating an LNER design from 1941, and built for the Sheffield-Wath electrification programme, which will commence regular service in 1952.

New named trains:
  "Merseyside Express"(London-Liverpool)
  "Comet"(London-Manchester)
  "Merchant Venturer"(London-Bristol)

The first Mk.1 carriages appear, destined to be "rough riders" in excess of 60 mph, until fitted at a much later stage with a wide variety of modified or experimental replacement bogies.

Sir Eustace Missenden retires from the chairmanship of the BTC.

H.G.Ivatt, formerly of the LMS, retires - the last of the Big Four's CMEs to remain in office with BR. After he goes, the concept of the Chief Mechanical Engineer is abolished for ever, being downgraded by the splitting of the post by creating a separate Carriage and Wagon Engineer. The WR, just to be different, has a Motive Power Superintendent.

New steam loco construction is 208 to "Company" designs, and for the first time the Standard designs have come on stream, 89 of them in all, of which 25 are of the "Britannia" class, of power classification 7MT.

BR staff number 600,000, route miles at the year's end are 19,357, and 37,000 new wagons are constructed.

Net traffic receipts are up £31.7m., and the surplus on railway working is up £35m.

114 restaurant car services are replaced by services of light refreshments, foreshadowing future reduced expectations of train catering. On a more positive note, the "Golden Arrow" does however receive a new set of Pullman carriage stock.

Again on the Southern Region, another main-line diesel no.10202 is delivered. Also, new suburban units with electro-pneumatic brake (EPB) commence operation - largely of the same design as earlier SR stock designed by Bulleid, they are however incompatible with them, and will eventually supplant them.

In August, the unions demand a 10% wage increase, but in the end settle for 8%, plus some concessions.

In October, there is a change of government. The writing is on the wall for the BTC, as the new Conservative regime will have little use for the concept of an "integrated" Transport policy.

In the same month, a Committee on Types of Motive Power makes its report, recommending:
  1) that diesels should be used for shunting purposes at all appropriate locations.
  2) the electrification of the Great Northern main line

should be put in progress straight away ( but in fact long-distance services out of Kings Cross will have to wait until the Eighties).

  3) there should be a trial conversion scheme of main lines to diesel operation, notionally involving the provision of 100 locos in the 2000 hp power range.

By the end of 1951, the BTC has taken over 3,766 road haulage undertakings - an ironic achievement, since the incoming Conservative government will already have its eyes on the future denationalisation of this sector of transport.

BR's accident record shows little improvement:

16th March - Doncaster - a Doncaster-Kings Cross express, negotiating a scissors crossover at 20-25 mph, is derailed, and 14 passengers are killed as coaches are crushed on impact with a bridge.

17th August - Newcastle Central - a departing electric train starts away with the signals against it, and smashes into the leading coach of an incoming electric train, killing its driver and two passengers.

5th August - Ford - a Brighton-Portsmouth electric train overruns a signal, and collides with another train. Eight are killed, and 47 injured.

21st September - Weedon - a Liverpool-Euston express hurtles down an embankment at 60-65 mph, following the derailment of the loco's leading bogie, in this case the result of poor maintenance.

Less disastrously:

19th November - Cocking/Midhurst - a bridge has been washed away, and Class C2X loco no.32522, hauling the Chichester- Midhurst goods, ends up in the gap. It will be more than three months before it is pulled out, re-railed and returned to service!

# 1952

The "North Briton"(Glasgow-Leeds) becomes Britain's fastest scheduled train, averaging a (surely none-too-impressive?) 63 mph between Darlington and York.

In March, the Light Weight Trains Committee recommends the implementation of experimental diesel-railcar schemes, as a way to solve the problem of unremunerative rural services.

The Ministry of Transport gives the BTC a Statutory Direction to freeze fares from March, pending an MOT decision concerning the increasing of "sub-standard" fares. Fares will from henceforth become a political football, subject to economic intervention by governments, and restraints on BR's market strategy.

The gap narrows between production of pre-Nationalisation steam loco designs, and the new Standard types - in 1952, 114 of the former, and 97 of the latter. Wagon-building amounts to 28,000. vehicles.

Further prototype non-steam locos are delivered:

1) the "Fell" diesel-mechanical 2-D-2 no.10100, ordered by the LMS, and built at Derby Works.
2) another gas-turbine loco ordered by the GWR, this time a Co-Co no.18100, built by Metro-Vick.

BR staff numbers are 601,000, and the route mileage is 19,726.

Net traffic receipts are up £37m., and the surplus on railway working is £39.6m.

In May, a White Paper forecasts the likelihood of a Bill requiring BTC to sell off its road haulage undertaking, as well as decentralising the organisation of BR, devolving more to the Regions.

Travel across the English Channel is provided courtesy of two new BR-owned ships - the SS *Lord Warden* (the largest car carrier built so far), and the SS *Normannia* (for the Southampton-Le Havre route).

Accidents:

18th April - Blea Moor - two locos hauling the "Thames-Clyde" express from Glasgow to St.Pancras are derailed at 55 mph by tender brake-rods striking facing points. There is considerable damage, yet nobody is killed.

8th October - Harrow and Wealdstone - - a Perth to Euston sleeper train, hauled by 46242 *City of Glasgow*, overruns signals, and runs into the rear of a Tring to Euston local . A northbound express,hauled by "Jubilee" 45637 and 46202 *Princess Anne* hits the accumulated wreckage, and 122 people from the three trains are killed. 46202 is so badly damaged (after only six weeks back in service after its re-building) that it is scrapped, a relatively unusual fate for a steam locomotive.

Two months later, the same accident nearly happens again, but this time fortunately no damage ensues. The Railway Inspectorate finds no fault with the signalling system - an Automatic Warning might have been of benefit in averting disaster, but little application of this concept has yet been made on British Railways.

# 1953

The large number of serious railway accidents since Nationalisation might have been less, had there been some priority programme of installing some or all of the following:

1) track circuiting
2) colour light signals rather than semaphores, at least in conditions of poor visibility. The SR sets a good example with much of its suburban network colour-signalled before the War even.
3) Automatic Train Control, whereby an audible warning is given to the driver, and the brakes are applied if it is not heeded.

There are two rival ATC systems in existence:
1) the GWR system depends on contact being made between a ramp mounted between the rails, and a shoe suspended beneath the loco.
2) the LMS system is electro-magnetic, therefore not requiring actual contact, but there is only one relatively short stretch in operation, on the main line of the former London,Tilbury & Southend Rly.

A full-scale experiment, using a version of ATC evolved by BR, is finally put on trial, with 54 locos suitably equipped.

The "Elizabethan" now runs from London to Edinburgh in six-and-three-quarters hours (still however three-quarters of an hour slower than the pre-war "Coronation" , and despite the fact of the maximum line speed having been raised back to 90 mph).

The "Man of Kent" comes into service on the route from Charing Cross to Dover, Deal and Sandwich.

The new bores of the Woodhead Tunnel, on the electrified Sheffield-Manchester route of the old Great Central, are completed.

They will have a relatively brief usefulness, as the route will eventually be discarded.

The decision is taken to extend the Liverpool Street-Shenfield electrification to Chelmsford and Southend(Victoria).

Not for the last time, the experimental schemes for railcars on lightly-used lines are dropped.

New steam loco construction: 28 "Company" and 123 "Standards".

New wagons: 41,000 (including 650 of the new 24.5 ton coal wagon - a BR Standard design, being the largest possible wagon to be carried on two axles, without exceeding the permitted axle loading).

BR staff number 594,000, and route mileage at the year's end is 19,222.

The surplus on railway working, which has been rising since 1949, falls slightly to £35.1m. in 1953.

There is an outline plan for investment of £500m.for railway development, including £160m. earmarked for electrification, and (bizarrely) £40m. for helicopter terminals!

Authority is given for the construction of 573 diesel-electric shunters over a five-year period, continuing the policy of eliminating steam in favour of diesel in important marshalling yards.

Between 1948 and 1953 BR has received 139 new diesel shunters, comprising nine different types (126 are diesel-electric, 11 diesel-mechanical, and 2 diesel-hydraulic), but not one single main-line diesel is on order. By the end of 1953, BR owns a total of 242 diesel-electric locos.

In May, the Transport Act 1953 stresses territorial devolution, and requires the BTC to set up statutory area authorities to manage the BR Regions under the BTC. The Act also provides for a Road Haulage Disposals Board to be set up, with the task of denationalising British Road Services, which will be the final nail in the coffin for any utopian idea of road-rail "integration".

R.A.Riddles, the designer of the BR Standard locos, retires, as does Lord Hurcomb of the BTC. He is replaced in September by Sir Brian Robertson.

The summer has seen fierce wage negotiations between the unions and BR management - after receiving less than their 15% demand, a strike is threatened, averted only by an agreement to implement the existing offer, followed by an improved one at a later date.

The Railway Executive is officially abolished on 1st October, and a period of confusion follows as to what is the revised chain of command and status of the railways.

Unusually, two maritime misfortunes for BR:

The MV *Princess Victoria*, a stern-loading car carrier on the Stranraer-Larne route, founders in exceptional weather, due to the sea smashing through the stern car-loading doors, and 133 lives are lost.

The SS *Duke of York* on the Harwich-Hook service is in collision with an American vessel, leading to prolonged litigation over apportioning responsibility for the accident.

1953's railway accidents are less extreme:

8th August - Abington, near Beattock - the down "Royal Scot" is derailed owing to heat-buckled track, and there are no fatalities.

15th August - Manchester - a Manchester-Bacup passenger train side-swipes a Bury-Manchester electric train (which has passed the Home signal at danger) on the Irk Valley viaduct. The first coach of the electric plunges in to the river, resulting in 10 dead, and 58 injured.

4th September - Stratford (the scene earlier in the year, on 8th April, of a rear-end collision on the LT Central Line, due to mis-application of the "stop and proceed" rule) - the leading coach of a train is derailed passing over facing points, is dragged along on its side, mounts the platform, and strikes an overhead gantry. Four passengers escape unhurt from this mishap, the possible cause of which is a linesman tracing a fault inadvertently operating the points, by touching together two terminals as the train is going past.

18th September - Guildford - a Waterloo-Guildford electric train crashes through the buffers of a terminal bay, killing the assistant station-master in an office beyond, as well as injuring six others.

# 1954

Steam locos constructed are 24 of "Company" design, and 184 "Standards", amongst which is Class 8P no.71000 *Duke of Gloucester*. Named in commemoration of the Duke's honorary presidency of the International Railway Congress held in London 19th-26th May, it is destined to be the only one of its class built, despite being designed to haul the heaviest and fastest passenger services.

A 2000 hp diesel-electric loco no.10203 is delivered, the last of a trio ordered by the SR, and built by English Electric and BR's Brighton Works No.10203's power is rated at 250 hp more than its predecessors.

Sir Brian Robertson decrees that Company liveries e.g. Chocolate and Cream for the WR, may be restored to a limited extent. However, the patient attempts BR has made in recent years towards standardisation of liveries will mean that little change will take place for some time.

In the London area, the Crystal Palace branch closes, along with its vast little-used train shed built for long-gone Victorian excursion traffic.

This ex-SE&CR line is anyway duplicated by an ex-LBSCR line running parallel to it, mostly less than a mile to the east. There is also adequate access to the suburban railway network at Crystal Palace (Low Level), which despite its name is still quite high above the general level of the surrounding area! BR will have to come to terms in the years to come with eliminating this kind of wasteful duplication - total route mileage is still barely less than that inherited at Nationalisation six years previously.

The BTC buys up the Ordinary Share Capital of the Pullman Car Company for £700,000, although the company is left under independent management.

Net traffic receipts for the year are up £14.8m.

# 1955

In January, the Railway Modernisation Plan is published - with a price tag of £1200m., "its main components shall be capable of being started within five years and completed within 15 years".

There is an initial decision to order 174 main-line diesel locos,160 with electric transmission, and 14 diesel-hydraulic.

Most are to be in the lower power range (up to 1250 hp , with only 20 attaining up to 2,000 hp and beyond). Orders are placed with a number of outside contractors, while in some cases BR workshops are involved in the manufacture of mainframes, bogies and bodywork. The plan is generally ill-conceived, and results in an excessive number of different types, with all the attendant problems of keeping a vast number of different spare parts, and training crews for a multitude of different machines.

Diesels already at work number 452, still mostly shunters. However, the English Electric 3,300 hp prototype Co-Co is undergoing trials, which will ultimately lead to orders for 22 more "Deltics" for the East Coast main line.

Steam loco construction continues apparently undaunted: 18 to "Company" designs and 156 "Standards". However, the big investment in the Modernisation Plan will be on diesels, £150m. in fact, with an expectation that this will add an £85m. per year advantage in the financial results.

£20m. is also earmarked for the installation of Automatic Train Control - now called AWS (Automatic Warning System).

Named trains come and go:

The "South Wales Pullman", an all-Pullman train, starts running from Paddington to Cardiff and Swansea.

The "Devon Belle" has never been a financial success, and is withdrawn.

ASLEF comes out on strike for 17 days - the resulting loss of £12m. in revenue is bad enough, but the length of the strike means that much traffic will be lost to Road Transport for ever. As a result, the year's traffic receipts are up a mere £0.1m. - freight traffic amounts to 274 million tons.

Although air brakes are the rule on almost every other major railway system in the world, BR decides to standardize on the vacuum brake for all future locomotive-hauled stock, on account of the difficulty of converting vast numbers of existing vehicles. The technical arguments in favour of the air brake are irrefutable, and all modern diesel and electric locos are fitted therewith, but for the moment BR ignores the inevitable price of progress, by delaying any radical change.

Accidents:

23rd January - Sutton Coldfield - a Class 5  4-6-0, hauling a York-Bristol express, takes a curve at 50-60 mph instead of the 30 mph restriction, and overturns as its train piles up behind it. Seventeen are killed and 23 injured in this inexplicable accident - although the train has been diverted due to engineering works, the route is well-known to the conductor driver of the train, and he is criticised at the Inquiry.

2nd December - Barnes - an electric train hits the rear of a goods train, and a fire results from arcing between the electrified lines. Eleven passengers, the motorman and the goods train guard are killed, and the cause of the accident is established to be misuse of the Sykes lock-and-block release key, by the signalman accepting the electric train into the goods train's section. The wooden bodywork of the EMU's leading coach is held to be contributory to the injurious nature of the fire.

# 1956

The first BR express diesel multiple-units emerge from Swindon Works, designed for the Edinburgh-Glasgow service via Falkirk.

In March, the BTC announces that electrification at 25kV 50Hz is to be the future standard on BR, with the exception of the geographically-distinct Southern Region, with its electrified third-rail network substantially complete.

Despite the above, electrified services commence on the Liverpool Street-Chelmsford-Southend (Victoria) route at a voltage of 1500V dc.

A working party studies proposals for a Victoria-Heathrow direct rail link - the building of the second runway is about to commence, and a quick decision is needed, so nothing comes of it. Passengers aspiring to a rail-borne arrival at, or departure from Heathrow will have to wait until 1977 for a Piccadilly Line link with Central London, via 19 or so intermediate stops.

Steam locos still roll out of BR workshops: 9 of "Company" designs, and 129 "Standards".

Freight traffic in "Merchandise and Livestock" has fallen to 85% of 1948 levels, mainly due to competition from Road Haulage. Bulk consignments of Coal, Iron and Steel are, however, still holding up well.

But BR's finances show for the first time a loss in net traffic receipts, of £16.5m. BTC would seem to be now in big trouble because of its nationalised railway operation, in contrast with other sectors which show modest profits, e.g.: London Transport (+4.5m.), BRS(+1.8m.), Bus groups (+5.3m.) and Shipping (+1.8m.).

In regard to Shipping, no less than three new ships for the Heysham-Belfast service come into operation, the "Duke" class of 4,800 tons and capable of 21 knots.

# 1957

"*City of Truro*", a GWR 4-4-0 built 1903, and arguably the first British loco to attain 100 mph, comes out of York Railway Museum to re-enter service. Having originally been withdrawn from service in 1931, it has been renovated to work principally on enthusiasts' specials, but is used on some mundane stopping trains as well, often between Didcot and Southampton.

The SR reverts to Green for its loco-hauled coaching stock, and the WR likewise with its Chocolate and Cream livery.

A Channel Tunnel study group is formed.

The former Great Eastern branch line from Epping to Ongar is electrified, and its running transferred to London Transport's Central Line - a single-line branch with the only level crossing anywhere on the Underground.

For the last time, BR workshops build steam locos of pre-nationalisation design, a mere 3 in this last year, making a total of 1541 Big Four designed locos built since the takeover.

Production of "Standards" is 141, the last year in which it will reach a three-figure quota.

BR's deficit for the year grows to £27.1m.

The Modernisation Plan is re-appraised, and the cost revised to an estimated £1,500m.

The Transport (Railway Finances) Act 1957 empowers the BTC to make borrowings to a maximum figure of £250m., for the purpose of covering anticipated deficits from 1956 to 1962, estimated to amount to over £68m.

BR Workshops and some outside contractors produce 13 new prototype side-corridor and open-interior coaches. The philosophy behind the designs is to move from the traditional concept of underframe surmounted with a body shell, to an integral style of construction.

Diesel-electric multiple-unit main-line corridor trains replace steam-hauled trains on the Charing Cross and Cannon Street services to Tunbridge Wells and Hastings. These units are built with a special narrow body-style for this line, due to restricted clearances in the tunnels (which had to be reinforced with extra inner rings of brick, as the result of a mendacious Victorian contracting engineer having skimped on the work). After a long and useful existence, these unique units will be replaced in the eighties by conventional SR electric MUs, after singling of the tracks through all the controversial tunnel sections.

In Hampshire, new DEMUs begin to replace steam branch services and locals. The Portsmouth area cross-country services, previously the preserve of 20 steam locos and train sets totalling 42 coaches, gradually receive replacement diesel-electric 2-car units, eventually requiring only 18 such units. With two less motive power units than the steam regime, the diesel fleet notches up 6,058 miles per day, compared to 2,587 previously.

A Single-Manning Agreement is reached with the unions in respect of diesel-electric locomotives - this is significant due to the appearance in 1957 of several new diesel classes:

Class 41 diesel-hydraulic 2,000 hp (D600 et al.)
Class 31 diesel-electric 1,250 hp (D5500 et al.)
Class 20 diesel-electric 1,000 hp (D8000 et al.)
Class 15 diesel-electric 800 hp (D8200 et al.)

Accidents:

7th January - Welwyn Garden City - a Baldock to Kings Cross train, after crossing over on to the main line, is hit from behind by an express from Aberdeen. The express loco (Class A2/3 *Owen Tudor*) is not fitted with ATC, and has run through outer home, inner and advanced starting signals, due to visibility being impaired by steam and smoke.

9th February - Chapel-en-le-Frith - Class 8F loco no.48188 loses its braking power (due to a fractured joint in the steam pipe)on a downward steep gradient, with a train not fitted with continuous braking. The fireman attempts pinning down the wagon handbrakes, while running alongside the train, without avail as the loco collides with the rear of another freight, and overturns with its wagons piling up behind it, killing the driver.

6th November - Lewisham/St.Johns - a Cannon Street-Ramsgate steam train rams a 10-coach electric train from behind, largely destroying the eighth coach. "Battle of Britain" Class no.34066 *Spitfire* is derailed, its tender causing the collapse of a girder overbridge, which crushes the leading three coaches of the Ramsgate train. Eighty-nine are killed (37 in the electric, out of a passenger load of about 1500, and 49 in the steam train out of about 700). The driver of *Spitfire* is tried twice for manslaughter, firstly with a jury unable to agree, and then acquitted. Poor signal visibility due to the loco's cab layout as well as lack of ATC (yet again) may well have been contributory factors.

# 1958

Following the number of accidents possibly preventable by the widespread installation of AWS, this feature of railway operation will be given a greater priority from now on.

Brighton Works, opened in 1852, ceases production and repair of locomotives.

Steam loco construction is 62 "Standards".

The decline in steam is matched by the rise of diesel, with the appearance of the following new classes:

Class 40 diesel-electric 2,000 hp (D200 et al.)

Class 42 diesel-hydraulic 2,000 hp (D800 et al.)

Class 24 diesel-electric 1,160 hp (D5000 et al.)

Class 26 diesel-electric 1,160 hp (D5300 et al.)

Class 28 diesel-electric 1,200 hp (D5700 et al.)

Class 29 diesel-electric 1,350 hp (D6100 et al.)

Class 16 diesel-electric 800 hp (D8400 et al.)

A Road-Railer vehicle is introduced, in an attempt to provide flexibility of freight movements between the road and rail sectors, but its take-up rate is poor, as the time of any serious any serious "integrated" transport policy has long past.

The traffic deficit of BR rises to £48.1m.

BR car ferries are a success, however, and are fully loaded at peak peak times on routes across the channel. The SS *Maid of Kent* with its drive-on drive-off facilities, comes into service on the Dover-Boulogne route.

Accidents:

30th January - Dagenham East - even the presence of AWS seems unable to prevent accidents, as a Fenchurch street-Shoeburyness train runs into the back of a Fenchurch Street-Thorpe Bay train. It is possible that the Shoeburyness train crew missed a danger signal in fog, but may also have cancelled AWS caution indications. Of 500 passengers in each train, ten in the Thorpe Bay train are killed, and 89 are injured.

19th November - Hitchin South - a triple collision in fog, with a down freight ramming into the rear of another, followed by an up freight running into the accumulated wreckage. All four running lines are blocked, and 34 wagons badly damaged or derailed, but the locos all remain on the track.

20th November - Milton - as trains are being diverted from the up main line to the goods loop, "Britannia" Class loco no.70026 *Polar Star* takes the crossover at 50 mph instead of the 10 mph speed restriction. The loco and its three leading coaches go down the 18 ft. embankment.

Less seriously, but inconvenient nonetheless:

In July, Class D49 no.62703 *Hertfordshire* falls over sideways into the turntable pit at Bridlington. A difficult job for the breakdown crane is the result, as access to the site is extremely limited.

In August, a relatively minor derailment at Borough Market Junction in the rush-hour has the effect of completely disabling the intensively-worked commuter lines in and out out of Charing Cross and Cannon Street.

# 1959

Ernest Marples, whose background is in the Road Construction industry, becomes Minister of Transport, and his Department's priority becomes the Motorway building programme.

Diesel-hydraulic "Warships" replace GWR "Castles" on the WR's crack expresses.

New steam locos number a mere 15 "Standards", yet diesel locos in 1959 total 601.

The "Blue Pullmans", built by Metro-Cammell, make their debut as six-car sets on the St.Pancras-Manchester service, and on Paddington-Bristol/S.Wales trains. They are designed to be a high-speed DMU train of luxury character, for prime business services akin to those of the Trans Europ Express being developed on the mainland of Europe to compete with international air travel. In many ways the forerunner of the High Speed Train, in having power cars at each end and being air-conditioned, these elegant units will only survive in service until 1973.

The first phase of the SR's Kent Coast electrification, on the third-rail system at 750 Volts dc from Gillingham to Ramsgate, Sheerness and Dover, comes into operation. The 4-CEP and 4-BEP stock built for these services represent the first use of the Standard BR Mk.1 coach adapted for multiple-unit running.

Electrified services commence from Colchester to Clacton and Walton on the overhead traction-current system of 25kV ac.

The 1959 Transport (Borrowing Powers) Act increases the £250m. of the equivalent 1957 Act to £400 m., a sum which will in practice be quickly exceeded. The traffic deficit for 1959 is £42m. There is an overall deficit of £84m.

The Pullman Car Company owns 195 cars, and works (under a contract with BR) 64 cars under BR ownership. It makes a profit of £83,000.

British Transport Staff College is set up at the former Southern Railway school at Gorse Hill, Woking.

New locos:

  Class 44 diesel-electric 2,300 hp (D1 et al.)

  Class 23 diesel-electric 1,100 hp (D5900 et al.)

  Class 22 diesel-hydraulic 1,000 hp (D6300 et al.)

An accident:

4th November - West Sleekburn - a runaway 22-wagon goods train, its wheels locked on greasy rails on a gradient, fouls the junction, and the crew of another loco are killed in a collision.

# 1960

In BR's last year of steam loco production, the total is only three "Standards", one of which is Class 9F no.92220 *Evening Star*, which is turned out in GWR Green, fully lined out and with a copper-capped chimney. The chairman of the BR Western Area Board catches the spirit of the moment:

"No other product of Man's mind has ever exercised such a compelling hold upon the public's imagination as the steam locomotive. No other machine, in its day, has been a more faithful friend to mankind or has contributed more to the cause of industrial prosperity in this, the land of its birth, and throughout the world. No other machine somehow is so human and so gentle, and yet, when unleashed, is capable of such prodigies of strength - nothing quite so graceful in action and nothing quite so romantic".

GW "Castle" Class no.4073 *Caerphilly Castle* is withdrawn from service, and after restoration to prime external condition, is transported by road to the Science Museum in London, to be on permanent display (some might say entombed).

751 new diesel locos are delivered during 1960, and the new classes represented are:

Class 45 diesel-electric 2,500 hp (D11 et al.)

Class 43 diesel-hydraulic 2,200 hp (D833 et al.)

Class 33 diesel-electric 1,550 hp (D6500 et al.)

Class 37 diesel-electric 1,750 hp (D6600 et al.)

Electrified operation (by locomotive and multiple-unit) between Manchester and Crewe commences.

The first phase of electrified services in the Glasgow area comes into operation, with 52 track miles on the north side of the Clyde. Unfortunately, things get off to a shaky start as the "Blue Trains" suffer from a series of equipment fires, and have to be withdrawn for modifications. For nearly a year, these services are handed back to steam locos to perform.

The Southend(Victoria) line is converted from 1,500V dc to 6.25kV ac.

In November, the suburban network out of Liverpool Street to Enfield Town, Chingford, Hertford and Bishops Stortford changes over to electrified operation.

Some statistics for 1960:

BR staff: 520,000
No.of stations: 7,450
Marshalling yards: 878
Coaching stock vehicles: 40,500
Freight wagons: 945,000
Traffic working deficit: £67.7m.
Net overall deficit: £112.7m.

Freight traffic is down to 249m. tons from 274m. in 1955. In the same period, new road freight vehicles have risen from 1.1m. by about a third in total number.

In March, Harold Macmillan says in the House of Commons that "the railway system must be re-modelled to meet current needs".

In July, the House of Commons Select Committee on Nationalised Industries reports, and concludes that 1959's losses of £42m. have been mainly incurred by BR's passenger services, mainly stopping trains, branch-line services, and lightly-used lines.

The Committee criticises lack of precision in accounting for the deficit.

There are substantial claims for pay rises on BR, due to a general acceptance of the idea of comparability between the wages of railway workers and those of other nationalised industries, as well as the public service sector, and appropriate private businesses. This brings the financial crisis of BR to a head, and there is a widespread feeling that the BTC should not have allowed money to be spent on "social" services, and that purely financial considerations should be uppermost.

A White Paper published in December, titled "Reorganisation of the Nationalised Transport Undertakings", proposes to break up the BTC, and re-constitute the railways under a British Railways Board appointed by the Minister of Transport.

An accident:

21st January - Settle - faulty maintenance leads to a "Britannia" Class loco no.70052 suffering loss of parts of its motion assembly. A freight train from the opposite direction runs onto the section of track damaged by 70052's errant rods, and is derailed alongside, tearing the sides off several coaches, and five passengers are killed.

# 1961

In May, Sir Brian Robertson retires, and is replaced by Dr. Richard Beeching, previously Technical Director of ICI, earning £15,000 a year.

Statistics:

  Route miles open: 18,214
  Total stations: 7,025
  Passenger journeys: 1,025 million
  Traffic working deficit: £86.9m.
  Net overall deficit: £135.9m.

New diesels:

  Class 46 diesel-electric 2,500 hp (D138 et al.)

  Class 52 diesel-hydraulic 2,700 hp (D1000 et al.)

  Class 53 diesel-electric 2,800 hp (D1200)

  Class 25 diesel-electric 1,250 hp (D5151 et al.)

  Class 27 diesel-electric 1,250 hp (D5347 et al.)

  Class 35 diesel-hydraulic 1,700 hp (D7000 et al.)

  Class 55 diesel-electric 3,300 hp (D9000 et al.)

There are new Pullman carriages built by Metro-Cammell for the Eastern Region's services on the Yorkshire, Tees-Tyne and Hull routes.

The electrified lines out of Liverpool Street are converted to 25kV ac.

A new drive-on drive-off ship, the "*Caledonian Princess*", comes into operation on the Stranraer-Larne ferry service.

The Great Western Society is founded, for the preservation of all things Great Western. Many of the steam locos still running on BR will eventually become working exhibits at the Didcot Steam Centre of the GWS.

Two accidents:

18th April - Pitsea - due to electrification work being carried out, there is single-line running in operation, and a down train is consequently proceeding on the up line. Trap points have been installed, but have been clipped open by mistake, hence derailing the loco to the right of the track, and the two leading coaches are telescoped.

15th December - Connington - a triple pile-up in fog involving "Deltic" no.9012, Class A3 no.60078 *Night Hawk*, and a V2 2-6-2, causing massive fouling of the lines by a huge pile of damaged wagons.

# 1962

As well as many other more humble classes of steam locos, 1962 sees the total demise of the remaining "Lord Nelson", "King Arthur" and "Schools" class locos on the SR.

On the WR, no.4037 *The South Wales Borderers* is withdrawn - built as a "Star" in 1910, rebuilt as a "Castle" in 1926, it has run a total 2,429,722 miles in its 51 years of service, an all-time record.

By the end of the year, the diesel loco fleet numbers 3,179, and there are various new classes:

Class 47 2,750 hp diesel-electric (D1100 et al.)

Class 17 diesel-electric 900 hp (D8500 et al.)

Class 73 electro-diesel 600 hp (E6001 et al.)
 (4 x 400 hp on 750V dc traction current)

The second stage of the main line electrification out of Euston, from Crewe to Liverpool, is completed.

The second phase of the Kent Coast electrification programme is completed, from Sevenoaks via Tonbridge to Dover, Deal, Ramsgate and all the branches in the area, 132 route miles in all. The only main-line in Kent now not yet electrified is Tonbridge-Hastings.

Southern Glasgow suburban services electrify.

In June, the London, Tilbury and Southend main line is electrified, and all steam passenger services are withdrawn.

BTC purchases the Preference Shares of the Pullman Car Company, effectively making it a wholly-owned subsidiary of BTC, and it is integrated with British Transport Hotels.

In September, the Transport Act 1962 comes into force, and the British Railways Board will replace the BTC as the body controlling BR, as from 1st January 1963.

Also in the Transport Act is a requirement for BR and London Transport to co-ordinate their services in the LPTB (London Passenger Transport Board) area. Also, the railways are to be operated as a commercial enterprise, with the freedom to pick and choose which traffic to handle, and to fix fares and charges accordingly, thus abolishing the historic "common carrier" obligation of railway operating.

Statistics:

Route miles: 17,471
Track miles: 47,417
Traffic working deficit: £103.9m.
Net overall deficit: £159m.
Freight ton-miles: 80% of the 1948 equivalent

Construction of new rolling stock is discontinued at the following BR workshops:

Horwich (locos)
Faverdale (wagons)
Lancing (wagons)
Eastleigh (coaches)
Swindon (coaches)
Wolverton (coaches)

and the 32 existing workshops are expected to be reduced to 20 within five years.

The North British Locomotive Company, starved of export orders, and with a disastrous record in diesel loco construction for BR, goes into liquidation.

An experimental 2,700 hp gas-turbine loco no.GT3, built and owned by English Electric, undergoes trials on a few main-line trains, but nothing conclusive comes of the exercise. It is nonetheless a handsome machine, somewhat resembling an inside-cylindered 4-6-0 with a streamlined casing and an attractive brown livery.

Accidents:

3rd June - Lincoln - a Kings Cross-Edinburgh sleeper express on a diversionary route enters a 15 mph restricted curve at 55 mph, and seven coaches overturn. Two passengers and a sleeping-car attendant are killed and 49 are injured, due to a conductor-driver's inexperience of diesel locos, causing him to underestimate his speed approaching the curve.

26th December - Coppenhall Junction - the up Mid-day Scot from Glasgow to Euston , diesel-hauled, runs into the rear of an electrically-hauled Liverpool to Birmingham express in freezing conditions in the dark. This follows a breakdown of the telephone circuit, causing the Mid-day Scot driver to proceed cautiously beyond a signal at danger, but then fatally accelerate when seeing the electric train's signal change from red to yellow. Eighteen passengers are dead, and 33 are seriously injured, and the lack of visibility of the traditional nineteenth-century-style oil tail-lamp is much criticised.

# 1963

The report conventionally known as the Beeching Report, but whose real title is "The Reshaping of British Railways", is published.

"Beeching" observes:

  1) in respect of 7000 stations, one half of that number produces only 2% of traffic.
  2) a quarter of total receipts are generated by only 34 stations.
  3) a third of the route mileage is carrying only 1% of traffic (in ton-miles and passenger-miles)
  4) half of the rail network does not have sufficient traffic to justify maintaining the track and ancillary structures.
  5) average wagon usage is a mere 45 miles per week of revenue-earning usage.
  6) out of a total stock of 18,500 carriages, only 5,500 are in all-year-round service, the others, if not undergoing or awaiting repair, being retained purely for summer or high peak services.
  7) 2000 stations and 250 train services could be closed or withdrawn on economic grounds alone.

In respect of closures, every case will need to be considered individually by Transport Users' Consultative Committees, as specified in the Transport Act 1947.

By the end of 1963, 167 proposals for line closures have been published.

On a more positive note, the Beeching report advocates adoption of the Liner Train concept, using both road and rail (sounds familiar?) for conveying containerised merchandise from door to door, in other words the forerunner of Freightliner. Trains of this sort commence running between London and Glasgow.

With this renaissance of vigour in the freight sector, coal traffic between pit-heads and power stations are planned to be run on the block train principle, known as MGR (Merry-go-round), to automate the conveyance of bulk traffic, by avoiding uncoupling and shunting.

BR happily reverses its former decision on braking systems by adopting the high-performance air brake as its future standard to be adopted. However, for the moment the wagon fleet is still largely composed of short-wheelbased wagons with vacuum brakes (if fitted with continuous braking at all!).

BR's Annual Report for 1963 contains a section called "Towards a Modern Railway", which attempts to show the Modernisation Plan of 1955, and the positive aspects of elements of the Beeching report, as being essentially in harmony, the latter being a logical continuation of the former.

There is a new plan for BR workshops to be removed from Regional control, and reduced in number from 28 to 16, and the workforce reduced from the current 62,000. Steam loco repairs are to be removed from Derby, Doncaster and St.Rollox. New carriage construction is to be concentrated at Derby and York, with Wolverton being retained for the repair of loco-hauled stock and diesel multiple-units.

The Offices, Shops and Railway Premises Act finally removes the railways' exemption from the Factory Acts. This in effect should improve the lamentable working conditions of many railway employees, forced to work in unbelievably Dickensian environments, with primitive canteen facilities, and shelter from the elements often provided only by structures that are little more than wayside bothies. The annual deficit of the British Railways Board is £133.9m.

BR-owned Shipping news:

The SS *Falaise* is the first drive-on drive-off ship for the Newhaven-Dieppe route, and its arrival makes Newhaven into a major vehicle ferry terminal.

The SS *Avalon* is one of the last conventional ships to be used on the Harwich-Hook night service.

The SS *Normannia* is converted to a car ferry for the Dover- Boulogne route.

A railway accident:

1st August - Norton Bridge - one disadvantage of AWS is its repetitiveness, and in this case a driver re-sets the AWS at three colour-light signals leading up to a crossover, double-yellow, yellow and red, before incurring a sidelong collision on the West Coast main line, after passing the red light apparently without realising its significance.

# 1964

The "Atlantic Coast Express" makes its last run at the end of the Summer timetable. Remembered by many as the train that took them to sunny holidays by the sea, no longer will its multitude of separate portions end up travelling down branch-lines to seaside resorts, many of which stand threatened with losing their rail access altogether.

Western Region "Warships" take over the Waterloo-Exeter line, Waterloo being the last London terminus for long-distance trains to play host to main-line diesel operation.

The BRB Design Panel is entrusted with the quest for a true Corporate Identity for BR. This will signal the ending of the Indian Summer of regional liveries for coaching stock.

The XP64 experimental coaching stock is put into trial service - the forerunners of the Mark II stock, they utilise Mark 1 underframes, pending the changeover to integral, or monocoque construction, whereby the whole carriage is designed as one entity, strengthening it to provide greater safety in collisions, and lessening of stress factors.

In May, the new Derby Research Complex is opened by the Duke of Edinburgh.

A new class of locos:

Class 14 diesel-hydraulic 650 hp (D9500 et al.) is destined to be one of the shortest-lived classes of all time, all 56 being withdrawn within five years.

In October, a change of government from Conservative to Labour means that Ernest Marples is replaced at the Ministry of Transport by Barbara Castle.

The total BRB deficit is £120.9m.

There are an increasing number of wagon derailments, largely due to the higher acceleration and running speeds of diesel traction. This leads to a temporary speed limit of 45 mph being imposed on freight trains. The BR Standard Mk.1 coaches are also notoriously rough riders, but not so as to bring their safety into question, just a poor selling-point for the comfort of rail travel.

248

# 1965

The WR is the first region to lose steam altogether (so to speak), as the last steam-hauled train leaves Paddington at 16.15 on 11th June, with no.7029 *Clun Castle* at its head, its destination Banbury.

The North London Line gets a reprieve from closure by the Beeching Axe, after a vigorously-fought campaign. It will not be its last threatened closure, as this part of the of the former North London Railway from Broad Street to Richmond will remain, in marketing terms, one of BR's closely-guarded secrets, useful to its regular users, but virtually unknown otherwise.

— HAHA!

On 31st May, Dr.Beeching retires from the chairmanship of the BRB, and goes back to ICI, from whence he came, and receives a peerage in the transition. He is succeeded by Stanley Raymond. ?

There is an exhibition at the Design Centre for the proposed new Corporate Identity programme, which is illustrated in a Design Manual. The name BRITISH RAIL is to be standardised, and the "double-arrow" symbol is launched.

Standard liveries are now to be:

Diesel and electric locos - Rail Blue
Main-line coaches - Blue, with grey upper panels
Suburban coaches - unlined Blue
Multiple-units - unlined Blue (with the exception of ER Clacton MUs, previously Maroon, which will receive Blue/Grey)
Station signs - Black lettering on White background
Brake-fitted wagons - Bauxite
Unfitted wagons - Grey

All earlier lettering styles are to be replaced by those of Corporate Identity.

New staff uniforms have been designed.

The only steam locos to receive Rail Blue and the double-arrow motif are, curiously, the three ancient narrow-gauge engines on the Vale of Rheidol Railway. All other steam locos will continue in their 1948-derived liveries until the demise of steam on BR.

The livery commonly referred to as Blue/Grey is in fact Monastral Blue and Pearl Grey.

BRB's deficit for the year is £132.4m.

There is a general mounting concern over BR's extensive fleet of fleet of outmoded short-wheelbase four-wheeled wagons, as they are unable to be operated with safety at the higher speeds envisaged in a modern diesel-traction railway environment.

# 1966

On 7th March, the main line of the former Somerset & Dorset Joint Railway, the "Slow and Dirty", from Bath to Bournemouth is closed. It has never had any regular diesel traction working over it, and in its latter years has seen some fine running by "Standard" 9Fs on passenger trains, over its steeply-graded sections.

Steam operation ceases on the Isle of Wight.

Steam is eliminated from the Scottish Region.

The West Coast main line is electrified southwards to Birmingham and Euston, enabling a full electric-hauled service to run from Euston to Manchester and Liverpool.

The name "Inter-City" is used for the first time to describe prestige long-distance services. The name is not exactly original, having been used previously for a now-defunct named train, but it is potent enough in marketing terms to be adopted by the railways of various non-English-speaking European countries as well.

Non-steam locos begin to receive yellow warning-panels extending over the entire cab-front, completing a process which began with "speed whiskers" and small rectangular yellow warning-panels, and "wasp stripes" on diesel shunters.

Steam loco buffer beams mercifully will remain red until the end of steam operation.

A White Paper on Transport Policy proposes a new financial framework, stressing closer integration of public sector road/rail services (yet again!). Heavy losses incurred in passenger service operation for "social" reasons are to be met from specifically allocated grants.

The Prime Ministers of Great Britain and France announce a definite decision that the Channel Tunnel should be built.

A subsidiary company SEASPEED is formed by BR for hovercraft operation - initially the Isle of Wight is the only route involved.

In November, ministerial approval is given to the merger of the Eastern and North Eastern Regions. From the beginning of 1967 the combined regional headquarters will be based at York.

BRB's annual deficit is £134.7m.

One accident:

14th August - Ardoch in the Nith Valley - loco no.D311, hauling the Carlisle-Glasgow sleeper, runs into a landslip and its train is mostly derailed.

# 1967

In January, "Britannia" Class no.70013 *Oliver Cromwell* is the last steam loco to emerge from a major overhaul.

1967 is to be the last year of operation for veteran LNER locos in the north-east on bulk iron-ore traffic. Classes Q6/Q7 and J27 have outlasted many of the Standard locos, due to to their rugged abilities in the work for which they were designed.

Ironically, the same year sees the demise of an entire diesel class, the North British-built D600 series.

The Isle of Wight's tiny remaining rail system is electrified, and uses stock dating from 1924, bought from London Transport. These curiously ancient units represent a creative solution to the problem of the island's restricted loading-gauge, but look rather outlandish divorced from their deep-tunnel context, and painted in Rail Blue.

The Great Western Society takes over the depot at Didcot, renaming it the Didcot Steam Centre.

New Class 50 diesel-electrics appear - a 2,700 hp design from English Electric (D400 et al.).

New locos in 1967 number 60, new coaching vehicles 482, and new wagons 1,590.

BR's annual deficit rises to £153 m.

Three White Papers are published: "Railway Policy", "Transport of Freight" and "Public Transport and Traffic".

The Labour government holds that the services of the rail system have "an economic or social value to the community as a whole which outweighs their money costs".

Research has led to the concept of the Advanced Passenger Train, incorporating a body-tilting mechanism (up to 9 degrees from the vertical) to minimise centrifugal force on curves. Originally planned to be powered by a gas-turbine motive unit, speeds of 155 mph are envisaged.

In June, the opening of the London International Freight Terminal at Stratford is blacked by the NUR due to a handling dispute, but the matter is settled after a fortnight.

8th July is the last day of steam working of the Weymouth Boat train, and from now on push-pull-fitted diesels will provide motive power, connecting at Bournemouth with the newly-inaugurated main-line electrification from Bournemouth to Southampton and London. The "Bournemouth Belle" makes its last run, diesel-hauled.

In August, a wages-grade pension scheme for BR staff is finally launched.

In the autumn, there is a dispute over guards undertaking second-man duties on diesel and electric locos. ASLEF works to rule, and there is blacking of some trains, due to the NUR breaching the terms of the Manning Agreement of 1965.

On 31st December, Sir Stanley Raymond resigns abruptly as chairman of BRB, following a disagreement with the Minister of Transport, Barbara Castle. He will be succeeded by Sir Henry Johnson.

Many multiple-units are now being re-painted in the full Blue/Grey, rather than Plain Blue.

Accidents:

28th February - Stechford - the driver of a diesel loco, making a shunting manoeuvre, mistakenly anticipates permission to make an unauthorised move, and moves from sidings onto the main-line. It blocks the diamond crossing in the path of, and is struck by, a Manchester-Coventry EMU travelling at 60 mph. The electric train is deflected to the right of its intended path, and there is much damage resulting from contact with overhead power equipment, and its driver and eight passengers are killed.

18th April - Roade - a broken wagon-spring causes a freight train to derail, involving it in a collision with an EMU.

31st July - Thirsk - loco no.DP2, hauling a Kings Cross-Edinburgh express on the down fast line, at 80 mph, slows to 50 mph before running into cement wagons derailed (due to their over-stiff suspension) from the down slow line. DP2 is a complete write-off, and 7 passengers are killed and 45 injured from the impact of the derailed wagons against the side of the train as it passes.

5th November - Hither Green - a Charing Cross-Hastings DEMU, travelling at 70 mph, is derailed at the third coach by a fractured piece of rail end, and all the following coaches are derailed. Undetected metal fatigue at the point in the rail where fish-bolt holes are drilled through it, costs the lives of forty-nine passengers on the crowded train, and a further 78 are injured.

# 1968

In January, there are only 359 active steam locos left on BR, confined to the north-west of England.

The Transport Act 1968 heralds a drastic reconstruction of BR's finances, with the following effects:

1) "Commercial" and "social" passenger services are to be considered separately, the latter to be grant-aided as long as the Minister requires es them to continue.

2) BR workshops will be permitted for the first time to manufacture for outside industry.

3) Infrastructure grants will be enabled for projects such as the Great Northern electrification.

4) The loss-making Freight Sundries business is to be handed over, with its plant and equipment, to the National Freight Corporation, which is in charge of British Road Services. This transfer of single wagon-load business to the NFC will enable BRB to concentrate on the freight activity it performs best, full train-load working to private customers' sidings, such as at NCB pits and CEGB power-stations.

5) 51% of Freightliner ownership is handed over to the NFC.

6) Passenger Transport Executives will be constituted in areas of major conurbation.

Statistically, the shape of BR is now:

Route miles: 12,434
Electrified route miles: 2,014
Stations: 3,235
Marshalling yards: 184
Staff: 296,000 (a 41% reduction since 1960)
Electric locos: 341
EMU vehicles: 7,492
Coaching stock: 19,500
Wagons: 437,412 (as well as 25,300 privately owned wagons operating on BR metals)

Total freight carryings: 207m.tons
Deficit on railway working: £90.6m.
Overall BR deficit: £147.4m.

The last of the Class 50 diesels is built, bringing to an end the somewhat painful first phase of BR diesel production.

"Kestrel", a 4000 hp diesel-electric Co-Co built by Brush/ Sulzer, is undergoing trials. Designed for 125 mph running, its axle loading proves too heavy tor BR's infrastructure, and the loco will be sold to Russia (undergoing a change of gauge in the process) in 1971.

The de-electrification of the Manchester-Sheffield route via the Woodhead Tunnel commences.

New employee grades are introduced:

Railman (replacing Porter, in the same spirit as Secondman has replaced Fireman in modern locos)
Leading Railman
Senior Railman
Chargeman
also Conductor Guard

An interim pay increase is awarded to staff in response to a non-productivity-related pay claim, but the unions reject it. The subsequent work-to-rule leads to the Penzance Agreement, a new productivity agreement, and the new staff grading system shown above.

In October, the new airport-terminal style Euston Station is opened by the Queen.

One of the most horrific and avoidable railway accidents of all time is that at Hixon Crossing on 6th January 1968. A 120-ton transformer on a

42-ton road transporter gets stuck, straddling the tracks on this automatic half-barrier crossing, and is hit by a 500-ton electric train at about 75 mph. The loco and the first three coaches are demolished, three enginemen and 8 passengers being killed, and 45 injured. For the first time, there is a full public enquiry, rather than an investigation by the Railway Inspectorate, and it finds that the driver of the transporter should have telephoned the signalman for permission to cross with an abnormal load, but in fact both he and his police escort were in ignorance of the regulations.

Twelve years on from the Modernisation Plan's policy announcement concerning the scrapping of steam traction, the last steam train runs, an enthusiasts' special from Liverpool to Carlisle and return. A complete ban on the use of steam locos on BR metals follows, and apart from a few private industrial locos (and a few owned by London Transport) steam will from now on be in the hands of the preservationists. From being serious heavy-duty revenue-earning industrial machinery, the steam locomotive will become a cossetted museum-piece for future generations, little more than a shiny parody of its former might.